By His Wounds

Meditations on The Passion

TOM KINGERY

WESTBOW
PRESS®
A DIVISION OF THOMAS NELSON
& ZONDERVAN

WestBow Press books may be ordered through booksellers or by contacting:

WestBow Press
A Division of Thomas Nelson & Zondervan
1663 Liberty Drive
Bloomington, IN 47403
www.westbowpress.com
844-714-3454

ISBN: 978-1-6642-6067-2 (sc)
ISBN: 978-1-6642-6068-9 (e)

Library of Congress Control Number: 2022904770

Print information available on the last page.

WestBow Press rev. date: 03/23/2022

But he was pierced for our transgressions,
he was crushed for our iniquities;
the punishment that brought us peace was on him,
and by his wounds we are healed.

(Isaiah 53:5, NIV)

Dedicated to my son,
Tim Kingery,
whose love and friendship,
help,
and family
have blessed me wonderfully.

Other books by Tom Kingery

Think About These Things – The Heavenly Mind

Supplement Your Faith – A Pathway to Integrity

You Need Milk – Not Solid Food

We Rejoice in Our Sufferings

The Letters of Jesus

Prince of Peace

The Ten Commandments Revisited

Introduction

But he was pierced for our transgressions,
he was crushed for our iniquities;
the punishment that brought us peace was on him,
and by his wounds we are healed.
(Isaiah 53:5, NIV)

His wounds. His pain. His suffering. He bled. He died for me. He spoke words of forgiveness, though, because "they do not know what they are doing" (Luke 23:34). Sometimes, I don't think we know. We don't know exactly what it was that Jesus did for us. We don't understand how it works that we could possibly be healed by someone else's suffering. But the stain of my sin and the pain of my guilt were cleansed and relieved because "the punishment that brought us peace was on him" (Isaiah 53:5, NIV). "The Lord has laid on him the iniquity of us all" (Isaiah 53:6c).

The wounds are God's wounds! Jesus Christ, the blessed incarnation of God, was crucified in my place. An innocent man suffered for my sins. A holy God bled when I deserved the punishment. A righteous Savior died so I could get away scot-free. He took the blame for my mistakes even before I made them. He suffered the consequences of my evil behavior. The accusing finger was pointing at me, but *He* was executed!

How could I ever make it up to Him? I feel as though any sacrifice I could ever make would be just a microscopic miniature of what I truly owe. But the only payback He really wants is for me to accept what He has done for me and to follow Him. "To this you have been called, because Christ also suffered for you, leaving you an example, so that you should follow in his steps. 'He committed no sin, and no deceit was found in his mouth.' When he was abused, he did not return abuse; when he suffered, he did not threaten; but he entrusted himself to the one who judges justly. He himself bore our sins in his body on the cross, so that, free from sins, we might live for righteousness; by his wounds you have been healed" (1 Peter 2:21–24).

We are called to follow His example. The closest I have ever gotten to another's being healed because of my wounds is by donating blood. A tiny little wound—a needle stick—and an occasional pint of blood, and maybe it has made a difference in the life of another—someone I may never know. But I'd do it again and again, believing it can help. I would do it for any one of you!

It seems like too simple a way of following His example. And though it may help to save a life, it will never save anyone's soul. Let's ask ourselves, *What is the sacrifice I could make that would, in some small way, at least, honor Him for what He has done for me?*

How about a sacrifice of time? "Could you not stay awake with me one hour?" (Matthew 26:40).

How about a sacrifice of money? "Do not store up for yourselves treasures on earth, where moth and rust consume and where thieves break in and steal; but store up for yourselves treasures in heaven … For where your treasure is, there will your heart be also." (Matthew 6:19–21). How can we do that?

Can I sacrifice my heart? "If any want to become my followers, let them deny themselves and take up their cross and follow me. For those who want to save their life will lose it, and those who lose their life for my sake will find it. For what will it profit them if they gain the whole world but forfeit their life? Or what will they give in return for their life?" (Matthew 16:24–26).

Indeed! And what can I give in return for the salvation of my eternal soul? What can I possibly give to Jesus Christ? For by His wounds I am healed!

The Passion begins, for me, in the garden of Gethsemane. That was where Jesus actually began to suffer for my sins. It didn't begin on Palm Sunday, as many scholars suggest. That was His triumphal entry into Jerusalem as He was hailed with Hosannas. It didn't begin during His last days before Friday. Those days were filled with teaching. It didn't begin at the Last Supper. That was a time of covenant-making with His followers. It was somber, but He wasn't suffering yet. It began after that. Maybe it began when Jesus said that His heart was troubling Him (John 12:27). He told His disciples this before His Last Supper, because He felt that His time (his hour) had come. But in my mind, the Passion is the suffering, crucifixion, and death of Jesus.

In this book, meditations on the Passion are offered. Many were messages delivered before the congregations I served. But like any other gallery where offerings are on display, I simply want to share my heart through the gifts I have to display. I did this with my sixth book, *Prince of Peace*, where the gallery celebrated Advent and Christmas. A gallery of paintings by a single artist may have different wings or sections based on style and subject. In *this* gallery, there may occasionally be different styles; there may be different opportunities to focus on the subject at hand through different lenses; and there may be similar images repeated with different settings, the way the gospel of John lifts different details than Matthew, Mark, or Luke. But the overall message will, hopefully, still come into focus. I know that I will not exhaust all the possibilities. I know my picture may not be perfect or complete; but, like a jigsaw puzzle, sometimes, when a good number of pieces are in place, the whole can be discerned.

I suggest to readers that it might be wise to read no more than a few meditations at a time. The images in this gallery are very heavy, but if we keep in mind the ultimate triumph at the end of the story, we can do it. Remember, we know there will be a glorious Resurrection.

May those who read these meditations gain an understanding of the Passion of Jesus. If anything, may those who read this book see my heart through these reflections.

Part I

As you enter this "gallery" of meditative images, here is a collage to set the tone. Beginning with a first-person narrative of "one who was there" and going on to the harsh realities that can't help but confront us when we consider the Passion, we begin to understand the plot and the tenor of our task.

There is a great deal of theology to unwrap as we look seriously at what Christ did for us in His suffering and death, hence the meditation entitled "S.C.A.R.S." We can enter the scenes of the story and imagine what might have been on the minds of the characters involved. You may think differently than I have, and that's okay. Just see these meditations as reflections of one person's heart. As earthly as it is, it has been inspired.

Put yourself in the garden of Gethsemane and wonder. What would it be like to be told you would desert your master? Or to deny Him? What did Pilate think as he faced his dilemma, and what could it have been like to watch Jesus die?

A First Offering

It may not always seem appropriate to blend several stories of scripture in to one *testimony*, but that is how the story shaped itself in my mind. This first reflection is a narrative. Imagine this: could it be possible that the "Cornelius" in Acts might have been the centurion whose servant had been healed long-distance by Jesus? And could that same centurion have been the one to oversee the Crucifixion, finally piercing Jesus's side with his blade? It would make for a powerful movie! And in my mind, it bears a wonderful message. Here's my first offering.

Cornelius

Now in Joppa there was a disciple whose name was Tabitha,
which in Greek is Dorcas.
She was devoted to good works and acts of charity.
At that time, she became ill and died.
When they had washed her, they laid her in a room upstairs.
Since Lydda was near Joppa,
the disciples, who heard that Peter was there,
sent two men to him with the request,
"Please come to us without delay."
So Peter got up and went with them;
and when he arrived, they took him to the room upstairs.
All the widows stood beside him,
weeping and showing tunics and other clothing
that Dorcas had made while she was with them.
Peter put all of them outside,
and then knelt down and prayed.
He turned to the body and said,
"Tabitha, get up."
Then she opened her eyes,
and seeing Peter, she sat up.
He gave her his hand and helped her up.
Then calling the saints and widows, he showed her to be alive.
This became known throughout Joppa,
and many believed in the Lord.
Meanwhile he stayed in Joppa for some time with
a certain Simon, a tanner. (Acts 9:36–43)

It's been a long time since I began to wear this sword. At least, it seems that way. When I was a younger man, being a soldier seemed to be a proper place for me. But that was many years ago now, and I have known enough of death. This blade has drawn ten times its weight in blood. But it never seemed to feel so heavy until after the last time it was thrust ... when I pierced His side (John 19:34). This blade. I hate this blade! It brings back such haunting memories. (I glance down at the blade in my hands and pause. Then I break the blade across my thigh and drop the two halves at my feet.)

Why do I remember things I'd rather forget? Why does my mind keep conjuring up the haunting look in the eyes of that condemned man when I came to the praetorium where the men of the night-guard were taunting Him (Matthew 27:27–31)? I commanded their attention, and suddenly, it was silent. Perhaps it was His last silent moment before the order to be crucified was carried out.

I walked up to Him in silence. "I must crucify you," I said. And then He looked at me as if to say, "So be it"—as if it was our mutual fate that the man who had returned life to an ailing child in my own household was then to have his own life taken away by me. And He was silent.

It's all still so clear—the exhausting road to Golgotha. The cross. The nails. The words He spoke. He even prayed for *my* forgiveness. But I've only felt forgiven when I remember the darkness of that day, when I remember the drink I offered Him from the saturated sponge, when I remember His final glance at me. There was a sad sort of gratitude in His eyes, ...and I was putting Him to death! I pierced His side. I crucified Jesus Christ!

Yes! I say Christ! Yes, I believe. That's not where the story ends. That evening, Joseph of Arimathea, a wealthy friend of a few of His disciples—perhaps a disciple himself—though secretly, because he was also a Sadducee, took His tortured body and buried Him in his own tomb, a cave carved from the rock in the side of a low cliff in Jerusalem. And then a tremendous rock was rolled into a grooved pit in front of its entrance. The next day was a Sabbath day for the Jews, and it was the Passover (Mark 15:42–43). The day was quiet. Jews were quiet on Sabbath days, but even more so at Passover. Why *was* that night different from all other nights?

I hadn't slept that night. I couldn't. It seemed so dark, but somehow, I sensed light. Deep inside me, something called. It still calls. I just kept the silence with the Jews. I think I even learned to pray. The Passover would last until the next day's sunset.

Early in the morning, though—too early—the chief priests and the pharisees of their Sanhedrin council, who had instigated the downfall of the Nazarene, came to Pilate. The sun hadn't even completely risen yet, and I could tell that they hadn't slept. I wondered what *their* prayers had been. Pilate hadn't slept either. I followed the Jews in to Pilate's audience. They told him that Jesus had said He'd rise again. They didn't want His disciples to have a chance to steal His body. They said that they didn't want the last fraud to be worse than the first. *They* were the frauds, though. I know that now. They wanted the tomb to be secured. Pilate was tired of them. He pointed to me, as if to order me, and told them, "You have a guard of soldiers." Then, looking at me, he said, "Go make the tomb as secure as you can" (Matthew 27:57–66).

I took two men who had had some sleep and ordered them to come with me to guard the tomb. They had seen the great stone rolled before its entrance. "Who could ever secretly enter there?" they asked. "Why would they try to steal the dead body of a criminal?" We sat down and I told them why. The day drew on. It seemed much longer than usual to me—maybe because it was just a quiet day. No one even came near the grave. I could have told Pilate that nothing would happen. The Jews knew too. No Jew even comes close to a grave on the Sabbath.

By about midafternoon, I couldn't keep my eyes opened any longer. I ordered the men to keep theirs opened until the third hour of the night. Then I would come and they could rest. I withdrew to some grassy shade nearby. Sleep was fitful for me. Dreamless. I woke up in the darkness a few hours before midnight, still exhausted. They reported that their guard had been quiet and that neither of them had seen a single soul. Then they went to lie down in the same spot I had lain, and I went to keep watch.

The only thoughts that filled my mind were of the day before. I remember how I looked at the blade that pierced His side, and wondered who He was. Water flowed from the wound I caused, and so did blood. I used my sword then just to make sure He was dead, but my blade was clean. There was no blood on it. It seemed brand new. I remembered saying yesterday what I was thinking: "Surely, this man was the Son of God" (Matthew 27:54). I didn't really know what I was saying then or why I said it. But that night, I wondered who He was. Why was I there?

I wanted to learn how I could live like Him because I wanted to be able to die like Him, committing my spirit into the hands of the Lord. But who would teach me? Why did I want this? Why *was* I there?

Then, I remember. It was hours before the dawn, and there seemed to be an eerie sort of light. It wasn't quite like a sunrise, but more like a piece of the sky piercing the night. I stood up, listening, my sword in hand. My heart was pounding. It pounds again even now as I remember that light. At first, my back was to the stone at the tomb. I wasn't dreaming. I turned around. The light was coming from within the tomb! My heart was kicking inside my chest. My ears pulsed with every pound. And then there was a rumbling sound (Matthew 28:2). I trembled, but not in fear. I'd felt an earthquake before, but it was different from this. The earth wasn't moving, really. And the last thing I remember before things went blank was a blinding burst of light as if the darkened sky opened up. It seemed to rip my chest apart. Then, there was darkness.

I was like a dead man (Matthew 28:1–4). I dreamed that I was dying. The next thing I knew was that before I found rest in my dream, the two men of my guard were shaking me. My eyes opened, but I couldn't move. I could hear, but I couldn't speak. "He's drugged," they said. "The tomb! It's opened! They must have stolen the body!"

Together, they carried me to my quarters. Everyone thought that I was dying. Later, I learned that they told the Jews what they thought happened. The chief priests bribed them to say that the disciples *had* stolen the body, but I knew better. I didn't die. I remembered the cross. I remembered the pain that Jesus felt. I remember His forgiving prayer as He was dying. I slept a long, long time, and I dreamed. What a beautiful dream! I dreamed that there was no death. And when I woke, I rose a new man. I ate and my strength returned. I looked on the world as if it was new. But I couldn't tell what I had seen. Every time I tried, the words just wouldn't come. My voice was stopped.

I went to Pilate. He was kind. Unusually kind. He wanted to reassign me to Caesarea. He told me to leave my home in Capernaum and move my household to this wonderful city by the Great Sea. I was to be the centurion of the Italian Cohort. I was honored. Caesarea was the port in Palestine where senators might vacation, where Caesar himself would sail should he come east. Caesarea was where Pilate lived most of the time. Duty was easy there. Perhaps Pilate thought I'd earned the rest. I loved him as my governor, and now he gave to me an honor just a step lower to his as the ruler of Palestine. His position was that of power, while mine was that of prestige. I wondered why he blessed me so.

And now I'm in Caesarea. And the reason for remembering my sword so darkly is that I heard just several days before that a man called Peter, in Joppa, a disciple of Jesus, had healed a young Jewish woman named Tabitha. They said she had died and that he had called her to return from the dead. But, like myself, I'm sure she was not really dead. I remember how Jesus had raised a child of my household from his deathbed only a year or so ago. He would have come to my house, but I insisted that He should only give the word, and the boy would be healed. His authority to do so was not unlike mine, I believed. I order an act, and it is performed. I didn't need to see it done. I believed He could order the healing, and that healing would come. My authority was worldly; His was divine. Jesus healed the boy. And now, His disciples could heal as well. Peter had healed Tabitha just a few miles south of here.

Tabitha was so good. Her reputation was known all down the coast. She had offered the funds to build the synagogue in Joppa. She was loved by the whole city. Her illness had turned every heart to prayer (Acts 9:36–43).

It was my practice, now, to visit the synagogue in Caesarea daily. That's where I learned the wonderful news of her healing. I gave alms and prayed as the Jews had taught. I studied their scriptures. I wanted, in every way, to be a good emissary of Rome, and I wanted to be a part of the land that Rome had come to influence. It's just that I thought the land should have as much of an influence on us Romans as we did on the people living there. I sought the power of God through prayer and kindness, rather than the power of higher office. Most of all, when I came to the synagogue, I prayed for forgiveness for having crucified Jesus.

One day, as I kept the ninth hour of prayer, I had a vision. It was like a dream, but I wasn't sleeping. It was more than that! I saw what must have been an angel. Its presence was like the presence of a great light. It was something so much more than me. A fear welled up inside of me. I'd felt this way before, hadn't I (Acts 9:26–42)? At first I was confused, but the angel spoke, and said, "Cornelius." The angel knew my name!

I said, "What is it, Lord?"

"Your alms and your prayers have been remembered before God." Then, the angel told me to send for Peter (Acts 10:1–7).

Who am I that Peter should come to me? Peter didn't know me, but he came. I told two of my most devoted soldiers, who were now part of my household, all that I had experienced—up to and including my vision of an angel. Well, I say that I told them all. Even though I had wanted to say some words about the experience I had at the disappearance of Jesus, again, my voice was stopped. I told them to tell Peter and beg him to come see me. They went the next day, and Peter came.

I met him with reverence. I felt so honored that this man, one of Jesus's closest friends, would come to me. I fell to my knee and begged him for mercy, but he lifted me up, saying, "I'm just a man"

(Acts 10:26). I told him my dream and about how I felt God's mercy. Now I wanted Peter to tell me everything he knew about Jesus Christ (Acts 10 23–26).

Peter spoke and told me of a dream that he'd had too. He saw a sheet let down by four corners upon the earth. There were animals, clean and unclean, together, and all were offered as gifts of God. And he heard a voice telling him, "What God has cleansed you shall not call unclean" (Acts 10:15).

Then I told Peter of my prior duty in Jerusalem and about how I was the one who pierced Christ's side. Could I be cleansed? I asked whether the water from my sword's wound could be my cleansing. I asked if a repentant sinner, an old warrior, could ever be truly forgiven by God. "Can I know more about Jesus?"

As Peter spoke, it was as if he was on fire with faith. Something deep inside of me was burning as well. Every memory of Peter's, every word he spoke was just like fuel. I felt I was a glowing ember underneath the ashes of a fire long since dead. His words were like a drifting breeze chasing all the dust away. Peter spoke of Jesus's Resurrection! Suddenly, I understood. And then, when he finally said, "Everyone who believes in Christ Jesus receives forgiveness of sins through his name" (Acts 10:43), the last residue was blown away, the embers deep within my heart burst into small flames, and finally, I could speak of what I had seen when the tomb was opened. My words were like a brilliant light, and I said, "I believe. God have mercy. I remember!"

Peter threw his arms around me, thanking me, blessing me, and praising God. He baptized me and all my house in tears of joy. I begged him to stay for a week, and in we went to share a meal (Acts 10:1–48). Peter said that whenever followers of Christ share a meal in His name, it is a time to remember. Remembering helps to make Him present.

It was a time to remember Jesus, share His presence, and celebrate His life, death, Resurrection, and the hope of His final return. So I remembered the last words of Jesus from the cross, and Peter remembered His Last Supper.

Now, I remember a decision I made that evening. I told Peter that I no longer wanted to be a soldier of the sword. I now wanted to be a soldier of the cross. I picked up the hilt of my broken sword, now in the shape of a cross, and said it again. "I will be a soldier of the cross!"

Enter the Gallery

In the entrance to this gallery, there is a brief collage of meditations. Most of these thoughts will be repeated elsewhere through slightly different lenses, so in a way, they are a kind of warm-up. Let them begin the impression of the whole, the way the edge pieces of a jigsaw puzzle help us realize the formation of the total picture.

S.C.A.R.S.

For while we were still weak, at the right
time Christ died for the ungodly.
Indeed, rarely will anyone die for a righteous person—
though perhaps for a good person someone
might actually dare to die.
But God proves his love for us in that while we still were sinners
Christ died for us.
Much more surely then,
now that we have been justified by his blood,
will we be saved through him from the wrath of God.
For if while we were enemies,
we were reconciled to God through the death of his Son,
much more surely, having been reconciled, will be saved by his life.
But more than that,
we even boast to God through our Lord Jesus Christ,
through whom we have now received reconciliation.
(Romans 5:6–11)

The cross was necessary. We needed a **substitute**. We needed the **covenant** of forgiveness. We needed **atonement**. We needed a **ransom**. And we needed **satisfaction**. S.C.A.R.S.

Substitution: Vicariously, through Jesus, we are forgiven. He died in our places. John said in his first letter: "God's love was revealed among us in this way: God sent His only Son into the world, so that we might live through him. In this is love, not that we loved

11

God, but that He loved us and sent his Son to be the atoning sacrifice for our sins" (1 John 4:9–10). Jesus took the sins of the world upon Himself. It was such a horrible a burden to bear on the cross that He felt forsaken.

Covenant: At His Last Supper, Jesus gave the covenant of forgiveness. "'This cup,' He said, 'that is poured out for you, is the new covenant in my blood'" (Luke 22:20). In Matthew, it is reported that Jesus said, "This is my blood of the covenant, which is poured out for many for the forgiveness of sins" (Matthew 26:28).

Atonement: The passage of scripture that begins this meditation from Paul's letter to the Romans tells us, "God proves his love for us in that while we were still sinners Christ died for us … we have been justified by his blood" (Romans 5:8, 9b). In the letter to the Hebrews, we are reminded that, "Without the shedding of blood, there is no forgiveness of sins" (Hebrews 9:22). This is why the whole sacrificial system was set up, inspired by God, to provide forgiveness through the sacrificing of animals. The sins were transferred to the animals, and the animals were killed, supposedly taking away the sins of the priests and the people. But animal sacrifices were insufficient. When the perfect, sinless Son died, He was able to take away the sins of the whole world. Remember that Jesus is described by John the Baptist as "the Lamb of God who takes away the sin of the world" (John 1:29).

Ransom: Jesus Himself said, "The Son of Man also came not to be served but to serve, and to give his life a ransom for many" (Mark 10:45). In 1 Corinthians 6:19–20, Paul reminded us, "You are not your own … for you were bought with a price." We became slaves to sin after the fall, and freedom from slavery could be bought. When we could not afford the payment, Jesus made it. We who believe in Christ have been set free from sin. "Therefore glorify God in your body" (1 Corinthians 6:20b). Peter said, in his first letter, "You know that you were ransomed from the futile ways inherited from your ancestors, not with perishable things like silver or gold, but with the precious blood of Christ, like a lamb without defect or blemish" (1 Peter 1:18–19).

Satisfaction: God required holiness. In the death of Christ, we are made righteous. Remember how Paul told us in Romans 5:9 that "we have been justified by his blood"? If we *are* justified, we *will be* sanctified! Made holy. Jesus fulfills or satisfies the requirement of holiness that enables us to then approach the presence of God without fear.

This is all just so much theological talk, Tom. Maybe the necessity of the cross is still not clear for everyone. But we can know, or, at least, I can know that Jesus took *my* sins upon Himself. He received the punishment that I deserve. He took my place. He suffered for my unrighteousness and for yours. His body bore the scars that would have been mine. That *should* have been mine!

He died that I might know eternal life instead of eternal death. His scars—in His hands, His feet, His side, His forehead, and His back would have been mine, but He took them instead, and I am free. He bled, and I am without the wounds. He bought me back from slavery with His own life. My belief in Him makes me righteous. My walk with Him sanctifies me. I owe Him so much! But I could never pay. Worthy is the Lamb! "Worthy is the Lamb that was slaughtered to receive power and wealth and wisdom and might and honor and blessing ... To the one seated on the throne and to the Lamb be blessing and honor and glory and might forever and ever ... Amen" (Revelation 5:12–14).

He is worthy! May my life always prove this wonderful truth!

Keep Awake and Pray

Keep awake
and pray that you may not come into the time of trial;
the spirit indeed is willing,
but the flesh is weak.
(Mark 14:38)

In the garden of Gethsemane, Jesus urges every one of the disciples to "keep awake and pray that you may not come into the time of trial" [lit. *temptation*] (Mark 14:38a), but they failed Him there. They could not even watch with Him for even one hour (v. 37). But they were urged to pray to avoid temptation. "The spirit indeed is willing, but the flesh is weak" (v. 38b).

At times, our spirits must demand supremacy over our flesh. Our spirits will know what our Lord wants us to do, but our flesh will cry out for its own fulfillment. There are times when sleep must be denied, even when we are exhausted, because it would be disastrous for us to rest at such a time. When the Lord commands you to "keep awake and pray," it is crucial that you obey!

As Jesus prayed in Gethsemane, He knew that the pinnacle of His ministry was quickly approaching. He was aware that the legions of Hades were marshalling their forces to defeat Him. It was at this critical time that He needed His closest friends to be undergirding Him in prayer. This was it! Jesus told them that He was deeply distressed, even to the point of death (v. 34). Surely, they would have sensed the intensity in His voice and the urgency of His demeanor; and surely they *could* have found the strength to honor His request.

But He found them sleeping. No excuses. They had fallen asleep at the most pivotal moment in human history, not once, but three times!

Jesus asks us to join Him in what He is doing. He may ask you to watch and pray for one hour. You may have to deny your physical needs and desires for only sixty minutes to pray with Him. You may even have to sacrifice some comforts, some other diversions, even something that might have seemed special, to be where Jesus is. Seek to bring every physical desire under the control of the Holy Spirit so that nothing will impede your ability to accomplish what Jesus asks of you.

The spirit is willing. Often, we think to ourselves, "Yes, I *should* honor this request, but ..." We compromise. We find something else we'd rather do. It is often like that on a Sunday morning or when the church has a Wednesday evening time of prayer. It is often like that when there are special studies offered and special services of worship.

One of the most relevant things Jesus ever said was, "If you keep my commandments, you will abide in my love" (John 15:10). I want to say that if we love the Lord, then we will abide in His commandments too. What do we do to abide? The branch abides in the vine (John 15:4–7). It does little more than abide. It doesn't strain itself. It simply stays connected, and that's how it produces fruit!

But a disconnect comes when the flesh is weak. The spirit is willing, but the flesh is weak (Mark 14:38b). This is a summation of the human condition. Do your best, however, to let the spirit do more leading in your life. And then watch how fruitful you become!

A Place Called Gethsemane

When they had sung the hymn, they went
out to the Mount of Olives.
And Jesus said to them, "You will all become deserters;
for it is written,
'I will strike the shepherd, and the sheep will be scattered.'
But after I am raised up, I will go before you to Galilee."
Peter said to him,
"Even though all become deserters, I will not."
Jesus said to him,
"Truly I tell you, this day, this very night,
before the cock crows twice, you will deny me three times."
But he said vehemently,
"Even though I must die with you, I will not deny you."
And all of them said the same.
They went to a place called Gethsemane;
and he said to his disciples,
"Sit here while I pray."
He took with him Peter and James and John,
and began to be distressed and agitated.
And he said to them,
"I am deeply grieved, even to death; remain here, and keep awake."
And going a little further, he threw himself on the ground
and prayed that, if it were possible, the hour might pass from him.
He said,
"Abba, Father, for you all things are possible;

remove this cup from me;
yet, not what I want, but what you want."
He came and found them sleeping;
and he said to Peter,
"Simon, are you asleep?
Could you not keep awake one hour?
Keep awake that you may not come into the time of trial;
the spirit indeed is willing, but the flesh is weak."
And again he went away and prayed, saying the same words.
And once more he came and found them sleeping,
for their eyes were very heavy;
and they did not know what to say to him.
He came a third time and said to them,
"Are you still sleeping and taking your rest?
Enough! The hour has come;
the Son of Man is betrayed into the hands of sinners.
Get up, let us be going.
See, my betrayer is at hand."
(Mark 14:26–42)

Imagine that you are about to jump off the high dive into a pool for the very first time. Imagine the feelings welling up in your chest. Imagine yourself wanting to go through with it and being reluctant to do it at the same time. You climb up the ladder to the diving board. You look into the water, and it seems like such a long way down. You're all alone up there, and you don't feel so sure about this. You can still back down, but you feel like it's now or never. You walk out to the end of the board, picturing in your mind exactly how you're going to jump. And now you know it's going to happen. But all of a sudden, the picture of everything that can go wrong flashes into your mind. You wince at the imagined pain you know you could feel. Now it's harder than ever to make the jump. You are determined, though, even though there's something inside you that still doesn't want to go through with it. It is almost as if there are two wills battling inside of you: one wanting to do it, and the other not wanting to. That unsure feeling seems to fade, though, the closer you get to the end of the board. And suddenly, the point of no return has come. The feelings of doubt are replaced by feelings of triumph. Here goes nothing!

In Gethsemane, Jesus faced his last temptation, his hardest trial. It was in Gethsemane that Jesus made his toughest and final decision. He knew this moment was going to come. He knew what he had to go through, and yet he could be prepared for it only in the way you might prepare to jump off the high dive for the very first time. But still, that's not the same. Jumping into the water is something we might like to do. It's harder to be prepared to suffer!

Perhaps it is more like being prepared for surgery. Knowing everything there is to know about the procedure is quite different from actually going through with it and going under the knife. We tend to want to avoid pain and suffering. We especially want to avoid death. The first law of nature is self-preservation. In Jesus, perhaps, it was not merely two wills battling against themselves but rather the divine law and the law of nature. He knew what he had to do: He had to surrender Himself completely. And He did.

There comes a moment when you are not yet at the point of no return and you're still second-guessing the decision to go through with it. It is as much a moment of doubt as it is a moment of decision. There is a flash of insecurity, and yet a sense of confidence is there. It is both a time of tremendous need and a time to pray.

You Will All Fall Away

How does it feel to think of your friends deserting you in your greatest time of need? Jesus thought it. What would it be like to *expect* to be abandoned? To think that those who have been so close for so long would back out and turn their backs on you? Jesus knew the feeling. The uncertainty was sharp. It cut into His heart and bled Him empty. He felt very alone, but He understood. His purpose was to give Himself up freely. The disciples could not be as strong. They were not strong enough to surrender. But they believed they were strong enough to fight.

How would it feel to be one of Jesus's friends, to have known the honor of being so acquainted with the master as to have Him share with you His deepest thoughts, His very essence, but then to hear Him tell you now that you will fail Him, and that you are unreliable, untrustworthy. Your master is expressing his lack of confidence in your dependability. Again, like a knife, it would cut you to the core. It would hurt in such a way that you would feel ashamed, guilty, and embarrassed. You would even resent the suggestion of your failure. And as self-doubt welled up inside you, you would ache for it to be different. Your self-doubt would turn into denial and denial into self-defense. *I am not unreliable!* you would think to yourself. You would believe you are able—that you can be trustworthy. Outwardly, you might speak, saying, "Not me! Never! I am no coward. Them, maybe, but not me. I would rather die!"

There is a determination in the human spirit that makes us want to believe in ourselves. We *need* to believe in ourselves. Self-doubt undermines that belief. Self-doubt is self- destructive. And all too often, we turn our self-destructiveness toward others and we fight. We are angriest toward others when we are angriest at ourselves. And rather than be angry at Jesus for exposing us to ourselves, we become angry at the ones we perceive to be weakest. "Even though all become deserters, I will not" (Mark 14:29).

A Place Called Gethsemane

Where can you go to let yourself be vulnerable? Gethsemane is that place in your heart where sorrow meets conviction and where distress meets desire. And each changes the other into a devoted sense of determination. It's where obedience is surrender, and the will of another becomes our immediate purpose.

Jesus was "distressed and troubled" (Mark 14:33, NIV). He

even admitted that His soul was "very sorrowful, even unto death" (Matthew 26:38, KJV). You can picture Him telling Himself, "Do not worry about your life … but, strive first for the kingdom of God" (Matthew 6:25–33). And the prayer He taught His own disciples would echo the phrase "thy will be done" (Matthew 6:10). Through His mind, there must have rushed a hundred doubts, and yet, He knew that "for God, all things are possible" (Matthew 19:26).

It seems that Jesus was his most human in Gethsemane. And yet, He was also His most divine. Could Jesus have been afraid to die? Or was He afraid not of dying, but of suffering? You would think that Jesus was about to cry. But it is not a moment of failure. It is a moment of judgment: not moral judgment, but a critical moment of determination. This is when Jesus takes His own great leap of faith. It may have been a wonderful leap of faith for God to come into the world as an infant in the care of very average parents. But it is so much riskier right here at the end, especially because His surrender might not be understood. The disciples on the road to Emmaus even admitted, "We had hoped that he was the one to redeem Israel" (Luke 24:21). How could God, who bears all power, relinquish it so willingly? People still don't understand.

In Jesus, though, God bore the weight of all my sins, of all your sins, and of all the people in the world both on that day and from that day onward. Could He have been sorrowful unto death because He also bore all that guilt? Could He have been distressed and troubled because He was at once God, so holy and divine, and yet surrounded with the burden of all the evil His suffering would overcome?

Surely, it was a time of desperate prayer. And yet, He was all alone. "Could you not stay awake with me one hour?" (Matthew 26:40).

I don't believe Jesus doubted God's power to raise Him. The cup He was to drink, the cup He was wishing to have removed from before Him, was the cup of death. Though God would have known everything there is to know about death, God had always seen it and understood it from the point of view of being alive. And yet now, God, in Jesus, was going to see death as a dead person! And God, in

Jesus, was going to suffer! Gethsemane is the story about God having to have faith in God. God had set in motion all His plans, and now God was at the point of having to trust in those plans to take care of themselves.

Imagine building a car that could steer itself. Imagine testing it. Imagine the inner struggle that couldn't help but come at the moment when you have to take your hands off the steering wheel for the first time. It's the moment of truth, when you have to depend on the truth to be in control and not yourself. In the gospel of John, Jesus told Pontius Pilate that His kingdom was a kingdom of truth (John 18:36–37). And in Jesus, God surrendered to the truth when he said, "not what I want, but what you want" (Matthew 26:39). It was the truth that would be in control and nothing else. But the truth is passive. It does not cause itself to be; it simply is.

We all face moments of truth. We all have Gethsemanes. It is not so much a decision of either our wills or God's will. It is a decision to let the truth be the truth and to trust it. And those moments of truth, when we must decide to go through with what we must go through, they are moments where faith is needed most. Sometimes, though, our faith conflicts with all that is still so human in us.

It is not easy to surrender. At the moment you spring off the high dive, you surrender yourself to gravity. It is only seconds of feeling unsure before you hit the water and go under. And the confidence returns on the way to the surface. And you're set free as soon as you rise above the water and take in your first new breath. It is only seconds.

But God, in Jesus, was facing two days of that unsure feeling before the stone would roll away and He would rise on the third day. What an incredible leap of faith He had to take. But first, He must surrender. "The hour is at hand; and the son of man is betrayed into the hands of sinners. Get up, let us be going; see, my betrayer is at hand" (Matthew 26:45–46).

Sit Here While I Pray

Have you ever watched someone pray? Did that person pray for you? Did he or she pray for another? Was the prayer for him- or herself? There's a unique feeling that comes when you witness someone going through something challenging and your heart goes out to him or her. You are troubled by their trouble. You are distressed by their distress. You are saddened by their sorrow.

Jesus told Peter, James, and John that His sorrow was killing Him. "Sorrowful unto death" (Mark 14:34, KJV). Was He sorrowful for their sakes? Did it hurt Him to think of what they would feel in the hours to come as He would suffer? Gethsemane can be a sad place, a very sad time.

It is not a time of fear, but rather of endurance. It is not a time of decision, but of resolve. It is not a time of retreat, but of release. Jesus loved life. It's hard to give up the things you love, even though you know you must. Gethsemane is a place of both resistance, denial, and acceptance. But it is self-denial, and it is the acceptance of destiny.

Gethsemane is also a place where we can be tempted to give up. "Are you asleep? Could you not keep awake one hour?" (Mark 14:37a). "Keep awake and pray that you may not come into the time of trial" (v. 37b). Gethsemane might be a place where the only escape from the inner struggle is sleep. It could be where the fatigue of the body is greater than the strength of our character. And sometimes, the body numbs the mind, and we cannot think to give an answer. Emotional and physical exhaustion, capped with the sense of regret from having been told they would all fall away, left them empty, drained, and unable to respond to any need besides that of enveloping themselves in unconsciousness. They could not persevere. "The spirit indeed is willing, but the flesh is weak" (v. 38c). What strengthens you in such a time?

It Is Enough

Have you ever been able to say that you have had enough? Have you ever been able to say that you have prayed enough? Enough is when there is no need. Had there been enough prayer? Had the disciples had enough faith? Had the need changed? For Jesus, the internal struggle had passed, and His destiny had arrived. For the disciples, the struggle of Gethsemane was just beginning. "The hour has come; the Son of Man is betrayed into the hands of sinners" (v. 41).

Gethsemane is now. Gethsemane is here. *Gethsemane* is when you struggle to face your destiny. Every commitment you make, every hope you raise, every desire you feel is a moment where destiny is at work to fulfill God's purposes for your life.

Gethsemane is a time and a place for grace.

The Humiliation

A certain young man was following him,
wearing nothing but a linen cloth.
They caught hold of him,
but he left the linen cloth and ran off naked.
(Mark 14:51–52)

Where would you go if you were naked and locked out of your house? Would you go to a neighbor's house, or to someone who knows you? Can you imagine the look on their faces when they open their doors? This time, you have not come over for just a cup of sugar! Or would you very purposefully try to go to someone who doesn't know you at all? "Pardon me, but I'm naked. Could you loan me some clothes until I can get dressed in my own?" you might say.

Either way, it's going to be at least a little bit humiliating, let alone somewhat scandalous. When you're naked, you're very vulnerable. People will wonder why you're naked, and there's probably going to be a few questions. But In this day and age, when so much of our personalities are identified by what we are wearing and how we wear it, to find yourself suddenly without anything to cover your body would be to find yourself quite lacking.

When Nathan, a prophet, told the story to David the King about the rich man who took the poor man's only Iamb so he could feast with a friend, David said he thought that "the man who had done this deserves to die" (2 Samuel 12:5). But then, David was exposed when Nathan told him, "You are the man" (2 Samuel 12:7). Because he had taken Bathsheba, Uriah's wife, and then tried to cover up his sin by plotting the killing of Uriah, he was no better than the selfish rich man in Nathan's story (2 Samuel 12:1–6).

It's terribly embarrassing to have your shortcomings exposed. In a way, it's very much like being undressed. To "dress down" someone is to humiliate them in front of others. Not only is there a feeling of embarrassment, but, even worse, there is shame.

To be naked is to be exposed. Being exposed makes us vulnerable. Not only are we vulnerable to humiliation and embarrassment but shame, and sometimes even disgrace. At such a time, we can be nothing but beggars, hoping for mercy and relying on the mercy of others. We are reduced to the simplest form of self.

When we are naked, we are not rich. Without our wallets, we cannot even prove that we are who we say we are; we have no keys, and we cannot open doors. We have no possessions, and we have nothing but our character. And yet, that may be put on hold a bit because it's so hard for most people to be themselves when they're so exposed. So, actually, we have little more hope than faith. This is how God sees us—naked and vulnerable. And you know what? God still loves us.

When Jesus was arrested by the chief priests, the scribes and the elders, and their band of vigilantes, the disciples forsook Him and fled. They had all been sleeping, and perhaps had even undressed themselves to be more comfortable, using some clothes as a pillow or as a covering. Since underwear, as we know it today, had not been invented yet, most people simply used a light linen cloth to gird themselves about the waist and between the legs. It's what Jesus is so often pictured wearing when He was on the cross. Because the common people didn't have closets full of clothes, they felt cleaner changing just this one article of clothing fairly often. It was inexpensive, usually not dyed, and easy to wash. It was probably about the size of a long bath towel.

Consider, then, this threefold embarrassment: First, this one disciple was sleeping through his master's most desperate hours when he should have been praying for Him and for himself. Second, when Jesus needed him most, he forsook Jesus and fled—as did all the others. And third, although he doubled back, probably hoping to recover his clothes, when he got close and realized that wasn't going to happen, he tried to follow the vigilante mob half naked. That's when he was seized. But rather than surrender with Jesus, he struggled against his captors, and—you can begin to imagine the scene—when they tried to hold on to him any way they could, they grabbed his linen cloth that came undone in the struggle, and the young man ran away, naked, leaving it in the hands of the men who tried to catch him.

I believe Mark reports this scene because he heard about it. Mark was not there at Gethsemane, but he wrote his gospel based primarily from what he heard as Peter told the story of the life of Christ when he preached. Maybe Peter actually saw it happen or maybe he heard about it later, but this scene appears only in Mark. And it seems like an odd aside, maybe even a bit of comic relief.

Still, imagine the humiliating shame the disciple must have felt when he regained his senses and realized his circumstances. He had failed Jesus in his anguish. He had forsaken Jesus by running away. And he had fallen victim to fear, the fear of guilt by association, only to then have to struggle with the humiliating exposure of his total vulnerability.

We are like that man. We may still be clothed in worldly attire, but we are sometimes naked spiritually.

We are called, as disciples of Christ, to put on the armor of God (Ephesians 6:11–17). When we are called to gird our loins with truth, we are naked because we are false, exposed by our actions that forsake the good that we would do, or, by your inactions, when that good is left undone. When we are called to put on the breastplate of righteousness that covers our hearts, we are naked because of our fallenness, exposed by the sins within that hardens our hearts. When we are called to have our feet shod with the equipment of the gospel of peace, we are naked, exposed by our failures to stand upon the principles of love and forgiveness that offer us peace. And then when we are called to take up the shield of faith, which can quench the flaming darts of evil, we are again exposed, naked, and defenseless because our grasps of the faith are so weak. And when we're called to take the helmet of salvation, we are naked, exposed by the fact that our minds are unchanged. We may think we are saved, but we do not think of God's kingdom, a kingdom of love and forgiveness, of goodness and grace, and of service and self-denial. A kingdom for all, not only for self. And when we are called to take up the sword of the Spirit, which is the Word of God, we are naked again, more naked than ever, because what we carry too often is the sword of the self and the word of the world. We don't even know the words of our Lord, which is not in our hearts. How then can we know of His ways?

How can we know of His ways? We can start where we are, in our shameful humiliation, because humility is the first part of repentance, the first part of change, and the first part of leaving behind all of the old life to put on the new. We cannot get dressed in the armor of God till we can stand before God, embarrassed for our failures, ashamed of having forsaken our Lord, and afraid of our faithlessness. Afraid, yes. The fear of the Lord is the beginning of wisdom. But fear is humiliating. But it's the humiliation we need. It's the humble posture that God requires.

Where would you go if you were naked? It's hard to accept the humiliation we are given.

The Release of Barabbas

As soon as it was morning,
the chief priests held a consultation with
the elders and the whole council.
They bound Jesus,
led him away and handed him over to Pilate.
Pilate asked him, "Are you the King of the Jews?"
He answered him, "You say so."
Then the chief priests accused him of many things.
Pilate asked him again, "Have you no answer?
See how many charges they bring against you."
But Jesus made no further reply, so that Pilate was amazed.
Now at the festival he used to release a prisoner for them,
anyone for whom they asked.
Now a man called Barabbas was in prison with the rebels
who had committed murder during the insurrection.
So the crowd came
and began to ask Pilate to do for them according to his custom.
Then he answered them,
"Do you want me to release for you the King of the Jews?"
For he realized that it was out of jealousy
that the chief priests had handed him over.
But the chief priests stirred up the crowd
to have him release Barabbas for them instead.
Pilate spoke to them again,

"Then what do you wish me to do with the man you
call the King of the Jews?" They shouted back,
"Crucify him!"
Pilate asked them, "Why, what evil has he done?"
But they shouted all the more,
"Crucify him!"
So Pilate, wishing to satisfy the crowd,
released Barabbas for them,
and after flogging Jesus,
he handed him over to be crucified.
(Mark 15:1–15)

Pilate saw through their conspiracy. Pilate knew enough about the chief priests and the elders and the scribes. He would have been informed about the religious ideas and ways of whatever region he might have been assigned to govern as a political proconsul of a Roman-occupied territory. He knew, just as any leader might know, that there were the powers that be, and the powers that aspire to be. He would have had plenty of experience with charlatans and rabble rousers, with pretenders, and with puppets. And he would know well enough that to keep the peace, he had to humor the status quo. Pilate would have known the significance of Jerusalem to the Jews, and, at the same time, he would have seen the self-indulgent pride in the insecure legalism of the local religious leaders. Pilate would have known real power when he saw it, and he would have known a pretender. And when forced to face Jesus, "Pilate wondered" (Mark 15:5, Weymouth New Testament).

As far as Pilate was concerned, the only offense Jesus had made was that He challenged the faith of the local religious leaders. To him, it was no big deal if someone wanted to be king of the Jews—they were obviously out of their minds. Other than that, he didn't want a rebellion. Pilate would have hated rebellions. That was why Barabbas was in prison. He was a rebel. He had fought and killed Roman soldiers in an insurrection waged by a band of zealots wanting to purge Israel of Roman influence. But Pilate quickly learned that Jesus was no zealot. He was a teacher, a reformer, and a prophet. So, Pilate wondered.

Perhaps a prophetic teacher might be a threat, but not a serious one. Not to the powers of Rome. To Pilate, the petty squabbles of the Jews of Jerusalem were more of an annoyance than a concern worthy of bringing before a Roman proconsul. It was something he just had to put up with. In a way, having to govern Judea might even have been considered a form of punishment for someone of Pilate's rank, but he was obliged to cater to their legalistic regulations. Doing so made for good diplomatic relations.

And that's exactly what Pilate was doing: He was attempting to use good diplomacy. As far as he was concerned, Jesus was no criminal. "He realized that it was out of jealousy that they had handed him over" (Matthew 27:18). But how did he know? How could Pilate read the situation so clearly? Was there something telling about Jesus that touched him and not the chief priests? Had he heard something? Was Pilate open-minded and open-hearted enough to sense the goodness of Jesus? Pilate wondered.

He tried to be as diplomatic as possible. (I think he could have been a lot wiser! But he was a pawn in God's plan.) If Jesus was popular among the common people, he might be seen as doing them a favor by releasing Him. He might win favor with the common Jew. Why should he care about the overly proud chief priests? But winning favor with the crowd would be a good move for the authority of an occupying force. So, because of a *supposed* (nowhere is this recorded in secular accounts) diplomatic tradition at their Passover celebration, he gave them an option. He could release Barabbas, a hateful murderer and an enemy of Rome *and* the elders of Israel, the Sadducees. He was the leader of a recent insurrection that made all Jews look bad, and who would probably incite further outbursts of rebellion and be arrested again or be killed. Alternately, he could release Jesus, a loving healer and a religious reformer, teaching a more spiritual way in the light of the current, burdensome legalism of the Pharisees.

You could compare such an option with that of a preacher saying to a congregation, "Would you like a nice, short sermon or a poke in the eye with a sharp stick?" Pilate was ready to go along with the crowd. And even though little good can be accomplished by going along with the crowd, it can sure feel good when you're accepted. Pilate probably needed the boost In popularity. The Gallup polls probably would have shown very low favorability of the people toward his leadership. But the problem with going along with the crowd is that it can sometimes backfire. Just as much as Barabbas had incited the insurrection that got him arrested, the chief priests incited the crowd to appeal for his release. I imagine Pilate suddenly becoming very confused and not a little surprised and disappointed when they asked for Barabbas. "What? You want Barabbas! You should rather want a poke in the eye with a sharp stick! What do you wish me to do with the man you call the King of the Jews?" (Mark 15:12).

Pilate's effort at good diplomacy was not working! He tried to save Jesus, but there was just no use. In fact, now, Pilate's efforts of using Jesus to win favor with the crowd were turning very sour. They cried out, "Crucify him!" Pilate asked, "'Why, what evil has he done?' But they shouted all the more, 'Crucify him'" (Mark 15:14).

Well, so much for diplomacy. I imagine Pilate may have been pretty fed up. This was absurd. In his frustration, he let Barabbas go and then took his frustrations out on Jesus by having Him scourged. He may have figured that if they really hated Jesus so much, maybe now it would be good diplomacy, and it would make him look even better to the crowd, if he punished Him hard.

I really don't feel sorry for Pilate. He knew what justice was, and he tried to serve it. He knew it was a conspiracy against Jesus. He didn't have to go along with the crowd. The closest he came to grasping the power he was dealing with was in his wonder or amazement. And now, history knows him as a pawn in the plan of salvation. He may have sensed a real power in Jesus, but he sure had a false sense of his own. Knowing the situation as he did, he could have banished Jesus to some desert island or something. Such would have been his prerogative. But instead, he had to go along with the crowd. It was within his power to put Jesus away until after the Passover. But by the powers that aspired to be, Barabbas was released to the powers that be, all in the service of the power that is!

Father, Forgive Them

Two others also, who were criminals, were led away
to be put to death with him.
When they came to the place that is called the skull,
they crucified Jesus with the criminals,
one on his right and one on his left.
Then Jesus said,
"Father, forgive them; for they do not know what they are doing."
And they cast lots to divide his clothing.
And the people stood by watching;
but the leaders scoffed at him, saying,
"He saved others; let him save himself
if he is the Messiah of God, his chosen one!"
The soldiers also mocked him,
coming up and offering him sour wine,
and saying, "If you are the king of the Jews, save yourself!"
There was also an inscription over him,
"This is the King of the Jews."
(Luke 23:32–38)

Vickie Sigmon tells of an experience she had one early Friday morning when a man at Central Prison in Raleigh, North Carolina, was executed. As the killing hour drew near, the men inside the prison, the inmates, started screaming. She said that to hear those screaming men in the darkness before dawn was horrifying. They screamed so loudly that the sound reverberated, cutting through the night and

33

into the hearts and marrow of all who could not close their ears. They did not cry out. They did not shout. They screamed.

They screamed and beat on the windows and on the bars and on the walls. And the screaming of a few was immediately joined by others. Gut-wrenching, soul-wracking screams. More and more men began to scream until, if you were within those walls, it seemed like the whole world was screaming.

The whole world *is* screaming.

Jesus Christ was executed on a Friday long ago. But for Him, when the act of execution was complete, He was still alive. After He had been nailed to the cross and the cross was lifted, He was able, in His excruciating pain, to watch others watch Him die. Two others, both criminals, were crucified with Him. They were also able to see others watch them die. After they were lifted up, Jesus said, "Father, forgive them, for they do not know what they are doing" (Luke 23:34).

For whose forgiveness was He praying? Was it for those criminals? Was it for His disciples who had abandoned Him? Was Judas included in His prayer? Was Pilate? The Sanhedrin? Caiaphas? Were His prayers for His executors, the Roman soldiers who had done the actual act of nailing Him to the cross? What was it that began working in the mind of the centurion who would later reflect an unexpected degree of compassion in the first moments after Jesus actually died? For whose forgiveness was Jesus praying? Was it for all those who stood by, watching, receiving some sort of sick pleasure from seeing someone suffer?

"Father, forgive them, for they do not know what they are doing" (Luke 23:34). The tense bothers me some. It is present tense. Is He looking at the soldiers gambling for His clothes? Is He looking at His mockers when He says these words? You'd think that prayers for forgiveness would come after the sins were committed. "Forgive them, for they do not know what they *have done.*" How can Jesus want God to forgive anyone *while* they are sinning? "Father, forgive them, they don't know what they *are doing*!"

Perhaps, the grace Jesus is invoking is a mercy so unconditional, so undeserved, so unexpected that even when someone doesn't know he or she is sinning, the person is already forgiven. Too often, we think of forgiveness as a result rather than as a condition. But here is one who is suffering for the sins of the world, for the sins of every single child of God living at that very moment—and living *since* that moment—and He's praying for the forgiveness of those who don't know what they're doing! What love!

We are not forgiven by His death, but by His suffering. By His death, we are set free from sin. And by His Resurrection, we are made new. All of it, together, is redemption. The one who suffered mercilessly has offered mercy. The one who was bound set us free. His suffering is what sinners deserve. His suffering is what we deserve. His suffering is what I deserve. But by His suffering, we are forgiven. "He was wounded for our transgressions, crushed for our iniquities; upon him was the punishment that made us whole, and by his bruises we are healed" (Isaiah 53:5).

The execution of Jesus was not surrounded by screams; it was surrounded by ignorance. The people who were present didn't understand what they were doing. Do we? Ignorance is a screaming sin when they would have known and when they *should* have known. But they chose to harden their hearts. Ignorance is no license for relinquishing moral responsibility because we *can* still sympathize with the one who suffers.

Every sin of ignorance is like a scream. If we could hear, we would be horrified. It's as if the whole world is screaming!

Part II

Part II

The Passion Narrative
of Matthew

In the gospel of Matthew, the passion of Jesus reveals very distressingly the utter aloneness of our Savior. He knew that He would be arrested, crucified, and would die but also that He would be resurrected. He knew He would be betrayed. He knew He would be deserted. He felt neglected at Gethsemane by His disciples who failed to keep vigil for Him and with Him. Friendless in His arrest, He gave no defense against the ludicrous accusations leveled against Him, and Peter denied Him.

Mocked, beaten, and abused by the Roman cohort, He suffered unjustly. On the cross, everyone just watched Him dying. Taunted by the Jewish leaders while the sky grew dark, He finally loudly expressed His forsakenness. The scenes we are forced to witness as we hear the story of Christ's passion are very heavy. Imagine slow, deep, ominous music through it all, with occasional loud crescendos blaring and shocking us to attentiveness. Our hearts are tweaked, and a somber compassion is inspired. But they also generate a deepening animosity toward the chief priests, scribes, and elders of the Jews. Even Pilate is depicted as having been conscious of their jealousy.

Through it all, however, we see everything unfolding as part of the divine plan. Prophecies are being fulfilled, and God's will is being done. There seems to be little mercy in the story. Not for Jesus. It breaks our hearts, but we know the end of the story, so we understand.

My intentions through these meditations, this "wing" of my gallery, is to bring to bear all that Jesus did for us as He suffered, bled, and died for our sins. The crucial reality of the Crucifixion is that it was excruciating. This is the crucible of the Christian faith.

The Mount of Olives

When they had sung the hymn, they went
out to the Mount of Olives.
Then Jesus said to them,
"You will all become deserters because of this night;
for it is written, I will strike the shepherd,
and sheep of the flock will be scattered.'
But after I am raised up,
I will go ahead of you to Galilee."
Peter said to him,
"Though all become deserters because of you,
I will never desert you."
Jesus said to him,
"Truly I tell you, this very night, before the cock crows,
you will deny me three times."
Peter said to him,
"Even though I must die with you, I will not deny you."
And so said all the disciples.
(Matthew 26:30–35)

The Mount of Olives is the place from which Jesus ascended (Acts 1:12), and it is the place where He and His disciples spent their nights during the last several days before His arrest. It was at the Mount of Olives that, on Palm Sunday, the crowds began to greet Jesus with *Hosannas* (Luke 19:36). East of Jerusalem, a short walk—a Sabbath walk—away from the city of Jerusalem in the time of Christ, the Mount of Olives was a place of refuge for Jesus. On a small plateau, on the western slope, in the midst of a beautiful grove of olive trees, there was a *gethsemane*—an oil press.

Perhaps the location offered an overlooking view of Jerusalem. Whoever owned the orchard must have been a sympathetic friend to Jesus, allowing Him and the disciples to rest there after sunset during the week. For many of us, there are places we like to be that just seem to give us peace. Perhaps there are sounds or scents or even a view that evokes within us a sense of calm or a sense of wholeness.

But not on this night! Already, Jesus had confronted His disciples with the harsh reality that one of them would betray Him (Matthew 26:21). It happened during their Passover meal. This meal is the Jewish meal of hope, remembrance, and freedom from slavery. It is supposed to be joyful. But on that night, deceit was in the air. One after another, the disciples said, "Surely not 1, Lord?" (Matthew 26:22). It would be the one who dipped his hand into the bowl at the same time as Jesus.

The bowl would've had either salt water or bitter herbs in it. Dipping a piece of parsley or celery into one of the bowls was a part of the ritual that remembered why the Passover night was different from all other nights. The salt water remembered the tears of oppression shed by their ancestors when they were forced to labor in Egypt for Pharaoh. The bitter herb was very likely horseradish, the bitter taste of which called forth the memory of the bitterness of their bondage. Either way, Jesus and Judas connected at this point in the Passover ritual. It may have gone unnoticed by the others, and it may have shocked Judas. But they all heard Jesus say that it would be better for someone never to have been born than to betray Him (Matthew 26:24).

Judas asked the same question as the other disciples, only, in the gospel of Matthew, he addressed Jesus differently. He said, "Surely not 1, *Rabbi*?" (26:25a). He did not say *Lord* as the others are quoted as saying. Judas only called Him *rabbi*. Did that expose something about Judas? Jesus tells him, "You have said so" (26:25b). Could that have meant there was something in the way Judas spoke, or did the question appear a bit too forced, revealing his duplicity? It doesn't say that Judas left at that moment. I don't think he did. I imagine Judas being at the table when Jesus blessed the Passover bread and gave it a new meaning. And likewise, the cup of wine. Judas shared the rest of the meal with the others, but his plans to betray Jesus churned away within him. They sang a hymn (did Judas sing with them?), and then they went out to the Mount of Olives (26:30). Was it then that Judas slipped away only to return later with those who would arrest Jesus?

At the Mount of Olives, Jesus said something else that would turn that night even darker. The disciples were already somber because they heard Jesus say that one of them would betray Him. Now, He tells them that all of them will desert Him. He even quotes Zechariah 13:7: "I will strike the shepherd, and the sheep of the flock will be scattered."

The book of the prophet Zechariah ends with an oracle about Jerusalem. Jerusalem will become "a cup of reeling ..." (12:2). It will become like "a heavy stone" (v. 3). But there will arise "a spirit of compassion and supplication on the house of David, so that when they look on the one whom they have pierced, they shall mourn for Him ..." (v. 10).

In the oracle, Zechariah goes on to proclaim that "on that day a fountain shall be opened for the house of David and the inhabitants of Jerusalem, to cleanse them from sin and iniquity" (13:1). On that day, God would cut off the names of the idols. (13:2) On that day, "the prophets will be ashamed" (13:4). "Awake, O sword, against My Shepherd, against the Man who is My associate," says the Lord. "Strike the shepherd that the sheep may be scattered" (13:7). Two-thirds of the people will perish, and the remaining third will be refined and tested. "They will call on My Name, and I will answer them. I will say, 'They are My people', and they will say, 'The Lord is our God!'" (13:9b).

In chapter fourteen of Zechariah, God goes to war, battling those who are against Jerusalem. "On that day, His feet shall stand on the Mount of Olives. ... And the Mount of Olives shall be split in two from east to west by a very wide valley ... and you shall flee ... And the Lord will become King over all the earth ..." (14:4ff).

But "Jerusalem shall abide in security" (v. 11). Could Jesus's quote from Zechariah have conjured up in the minds of the disciples those oracles? Did they even know the prophetic proclamations?

I don't think so. Peter took it all personally. "Even though all the rest become deserters because of You, I will never desert You" (Matthew 26:33). We would all profess the same loyalty. And yet, we all desert Him when we profess faith and fail to defend it, when we claim to know the truth and yet we listen to little lies, or when we think we're deep and yet we rarely go beneath the surface! The rift in the Mount of Olives will divide the true believers from the nominal followers; the spirit-filled from the hard-hearted; the compassionate from the apathetic; the serious from the complacent.

"Truly I tell you, this very night, before the cock crows, you will deny me three times" (26:34). "Even though I must die with you, I will not deny You!" And so said all the rest (v. 35). And all of them failed.

May we never fail in such a way!

I Will Never Desert You

When they had sung the hymn, they went
out to the Mount of Olives.
Then Jesus said to them,
"You will all become deserters because of this night;
for it is written,
'I will strike the shepherd, and the sheep
of the flock will be scattered.'
But after I am raised up, I will go ahead of you to Galilee."
Peter said to him,
"Though all become deserters because of
you, I will never desert you."
Jesus said to him,
"Truly I tell you, this very night,
before the cock crows, you will deny me three times."
Peter said to him,
"Even though I must die with you,
I will not deny you."
And so said all the disciples.
(Matthew 26:30–35)

Overconfidence? Questions and possible clues to reasons for the disciples' overconfidence are easy to discern. Did they think that somehow, a special part of the Passover meal would (or had) endow(ed) them with some sort of supernatural strength or ability to become great warriors in a battle that would establish Jesus as king in Israel? Did the idea that symbolically eating the body and drinking the blood of Jesus would infuse them with a sense of righteousness so pure and so perfect that they would be considered as qualifying as generals in some kind of divine army? Did calling the cup of wine "My blood of the covenant" (Matthew 26:28) give them (or at least Peter) a sense of their being initiated into a special order of faithful devotees who would reign with Christ in His great kingdom?

Several chapters earlier, we get a clue:

> "Look, we have left everything and followed you. What are we to have?" Jesus said to them, "Truly I tell you, at the renewal of all things, when the Son of Man is seated on the throne of his glory, you who have followed me will also sit on twelve thrones, judging the twelve tribes of Israel. And everyone who has left houses or brothers or sisters or father or mother or children, or fields, for my name's sake, will receive a hundredfold, and will inherit eternal life. But many who are first will be last, and the last will be first." (Matthew 19:27–30)

Did Jesus telling them, "I will never again drink of this fruit of the vine until the day when I drink it new with you in my Father's kingdom" (Matthew 26:29) give them a sense of immanence as if that night, or, by dawn, the battle would begin, and the kingdom would come? If you can imagine the thoughts of the disciples leaning to any degree in these directions, you can understand the vehemence with which Peter spoke when he said, "'Even though I must die with you, I will not deny you.' And so said all the disciples" (Matthew 26:35).

After their Passover meal, they sang a hymn—probably one of the praise Psalms from Psalms 113 to 118—and then they walked the half mile or so to the Mount of Olives where they were going to spend the night in the open air under the stars near the olive press, the *gethsemane*. I picture them sitting in a circle around a small bonfire where its flames barely illumined each man's face, while Jesus says, "You will all become deserters because of this night" (Matthew 26:31).

Jesus *had* told them several times that He would be arrested, tried, mocked, beaten, and crucified. Did they think that, somehow, perhaps, just before His moment of death, when Jesus was most vulnerable and weak, that He would suddenly reverse it all and the great battle would begin? Such defeatist talk from Jesus seemed anything but appropriate at the moment. Maybe the disciples could already taste the victory! They could feel the glory of the kingdom. The moment for them to shine was upon them, not to run away.

And Peter said, "Even though they all become deserters, I will never desert you" (Matthew 26:33). How bold of him—and how condescending to all the others. They were never going to leave their rabbi, their master, their Lord! (Did any of them notice that Judas was missing from the group?) In my mind, Peter is not trying to be condescending; he is saying what he says to rally them, to get them all to sign on with him. His words are meant to be encouraging, not insulting. After all, it had the effect of them adding to Peter's claim that he would never deny Jesus, especially not three times! And maybe, just maybe, they had never lost the visionary image of what Jesus had said to them earlier about them sitting on thrones with Him.

So with great confidence, they all proclaimed their loyalty. How could they possibly fail their master or forsake Him at such a world-altering time as this? How could anyone desert Christ after all He had done for them? How could they choose not to worship Him, to honor Him, to let their lights shine in such a way as to give God glory? We practice the remembrance of Christ every time we reenact His Last Supper! How could anyone ever act as though he or she had forgotten Him?

Do we become overconfident the way Peter did, the way they all did? Do we think we are any better than they were on that night? Of course we do! We have His Spirit! We would never forsake our Lord. Never!

The Vigil

Then Jesus went with them to a place called Gethsemane;
and he said to his disciples,
"Sit here while I go over there and pray."
He took with him Peter and the two sons of Zebedee,
and began to be grieved and agitated.
Then he said to them,
"I am deeply grieved, even to the point of death;
remain here, and stay awake with me."
And going a little farther, he threw himself
on the ground and prayed,
"My Father, if it is possible, let this cup pass from me;
yet not what I want but what you want."
Then he came to the disciples and found them sleeping;
and he said to Peter,
"So could you not stay awake with me one hour?
Stay awake and pray that you may not come into the time of trial;
the spirit indeed is willing, but the flesh is weak."
Again he went away for the second time and prayed,
"My Father, if this cannot pass unless I drink it, your will be done."
Again he came and found them sleeping, for their eyes were heavy.
So leaving them again, he went away and prayed for the third time,
saying the same words.
Then he came to the disciples and said to them,
"Are you still sleeping and taking your rest?
See, the hour is at hand,

and the Son of Man is betrayed into the hands of sinners.
Get up,
let us be going.
See, my betrayer is at hand."
(Matthew 26:36–46)

The word *gethsemane* means *oil press*. You can imagine the laborers gathering the olives and bringing them to this place. The olives would be placed in large, mesh-like bags, through which the oil could drip to a funnel carved in the stone press, beneath which, a clay jar could collect the clear, golden liquid. The leftover mash of olives would be fed to the goats. But in order to press the olives, there would be a thick, strong board wedged over the bags of olives. At the outside end of this board, heavy stones would be tied. The board would press down hard on the olives, crushing the meat of the fruit, squeezing its juices out, and producing the olive oil.

It seems a bitter parallel to what was happening to Jesus at the time. "I am deeply grieved, even to the point of death. Remain here, and stay awake with me" (Matthew 26:38). The weight of the world was pressing down on Jesus, and He was distressed. He didn't want to be alone. Peter, James, and John were asked to sit nearby, not so much to be on guard as to just be there—to just stay awake with Him. They were also the ones who were selected to be with Christ when He was transfigured! (Matthew 17:1–8).

Through the darkness of this night, the pain of *my* guilt and the stain of *my* sin was being placed on my Lord. Jesus knew He was going to suffer for my sins that I might be made righteous before God. He was innocent, and yet He was going to die for me. He was going to take the punishment I deserve. He was beaten, flogged, and crucified in my place.

He prayed that this cup of suffering might not have to be taken. And still, He knew His purpose, and so He prayed the purest prayer of surrender: "Not what I want, but what you want … My Father" (v. 39). These were not the only prayers He prayed through those hours. John recorded some of what he heard Jesus saying to God in *his* gospel (chapter 17). But here, in the vigil of our Lord, Matthew records Christ's deepest anguish.

Meanwhile, Judas had gone off to betray Him by leading the powers that be to His location, even though it was never really secret. Jesus knew that soon the rest of the disciples would desert Him too. He knew He was going to be crucified. But He also knew He would be raised from the dead. That knowledge brought His surrender a bit of sweetness. There was light in His darkness, but that darkness was very, very deep. Only Luke mentions the true depth of Christ's despair within that darkness. He told of how an angel came to strengthen Him as he prayed more earnestly, and "his sweat became like great drops of blood" (Luke 22:43–44).

He needed His friends. So alone that it hurt, He came to Peter, James, and John, and they were sleeping. It was not disappointment that He was expressing when He said, "So could you not stay awake with me one hour?" (v. 40). It was simply a recognition of how He was more alone than He wanted to be. He tried to encourage them, telling them to keep vigil in order to escape temptation (v. 41a). I'm not sure what temptations Jesus might have been thinking about. Is it a temptation to sleep? Is it a temptation for them to have deserted their post? Or could it have been a temptation to ignore the gravity of that night?

And then, Jesus made the statement that reveals the divine understanding of human nature: "The spirit indeed is willing, but the flesh is weak" (v. 41b).

Jesus went back to His place of prayer and prayed again: "My Father, if this cup cannot pass unless I drink it, your will be done" (v. 42). This wasn't easy for Jesus. Even though He is God-incarnate, even though He is the anointed Son of God, He was taking my guilt into Himself—my sin, my unrighteousness—and it was weighing heavily on His heart.

"Their eyes were heavy" (v. 43). He knew they would fail Him, but please, not yet! Not until His arrest, not until the threat came. Not until *Judas* showed up. All Jesus wanted was for His three closest disciples to stay awake with Him just so He wouldn't feel so alone.

After finding them asleep a second time, He said nothing, but simply returned to His prayers, praying as He had before (v. 44).

Jesus knew what was about to happen. Maybe He sensed it before He saw it. Sometimes evil and malice can be felt. Jesus came again to Peter, James, and John after praying a third time. They were still sleeping, but the time had come. "The Son of Man is betrayed into the hands of sinners" (v. 45). Of course, *they* didn't think they were sinners. These Jews, leaders of the faith, thought they were doing a good thing—defending Judaism against a "false" messiah. But they were blinded by their status, their positions before the people, and their power. Jesus had told them so. Only days before, He proclaimed their hypocrisy through a litany of seven woes against the scribes and Pharisees (Matthew 23:13–36). They hated Him for it, but He wasn't telling them anything the people weren't already thinking. From Christ's point of view, the chosen one, the anointed one, the Son of Man, *they* were sinners.

They were coming from Jerusalem. It was dark. The fire of torchlight guided their path. Was Judas leading them? From the overlook of Gethsemane, Jesus could see them coming. "'Get up,' He said. 'Let us be going. See, my betrayer is at hand'" (v. 46).

He could see Judas. Jesus was about to be arrested.

There comes a time when we need to deepen our conviction, when we need to defend ourselves as we say, "Surely, not I, Lord" (Matthew 26:23). We all need to examine our lives and see wherein we are betraying our Lord and deserting Him. Are our journeys going in the right direction? Is each of our character being fashioned after the example of Christ? Are we surrendered? Are we faithful to the extent that we are being made perfect in love?

The spirit is willing!

The Arrest and Desertion

While he was still speaking,
Judas, one of the twelve, arrived;
with him was a large crowd with swords and clubs,
from the chief priests and the elders of the people.
Now the betrayer had given them a sign,
saying, "The one I will kiss is the man; arrest him."
At once he came up to Jesus and said,
"Greetings, Rabbi!"
and kissed him.
Jesus said to him,
"Friend, do what you are here to do."
Then they came and laid hands on Jesus and arrested him.
Suddenly, one of those with Jesus put his hand on his sword,
drew it, and struck the slave of the high priest, cutting off his ear.
Then Jesus said to him,
"Put your sword back in its place;
for all who take the sword will perish by the sword.
Do you not think that I cannot appeal to my Father,
and he will at once send me more than twelve legions of angels?
But how then would the scriptures be fulfilled,
which say it must happen this way?"
At that hour Jesus said to the crowds,
"Have you come out with swords and clubs to arrest me
as though I were a bandit?
Day after day

> I sat in the temple teaching,
> and you did not arrest me.
> But all this has taken place,
> so that the scriptures of the prophets may be fulfilled."
> Then all his disciples deserted him and fled.
> (Matthew 26:47–56)

Some stories have several points of climax. The Palm Sunday procession was the first one. I believe the arrest is the second. Jesus had been speaking to Peter, James, and John. "The hour is at hand, and the Son of Man is betrayed into the hands of sinners. Get up. Let us be going. See, my betrayer is at hand" (26:45b–46). Jesus could see the face of Judas in the torchlight.

And "While He was speaking, Judas arrived" (v. 47a). We know where he's been by knowing who's with him: "A large crowd with swords and clubs ... from the chief priests and the elders of the people" (v. 47b). There was no doubt about what was going on, and there was no doubt about who was betraying Jesus. Judas had even told them that he would embrace with affection the One they were to arrest. (v. 48) Why Judas did what he did is not really known. Neither are the details able to give us enough clues. We can only speculate.

So, this is only speculation: the name *Iscariot*—Judas is the only disciple with a last name—may give a clue. It could simply mean *from Kerioth*, a town in Israel. But it could also mean a *sicarii*. A sicarius was a short, sharp blade with a solid, firm handle. It was sometimes used by radical zealots. They could blend into a crowd of people, sneak up to a Roman soldier, stab him quickly, and be long gone from the spot before the dead person hit the ground.

Such radical zealots, *sicarii*—sicarius-wielders—were eager for the time of revolt to come. A zealot was someone who was zealous for the kingdom of Israel, especially for their land to be rid of their pagan occupiers. They claimed a fervent patriotism, but not a serious faith. They simply hated the Romans. A sicarii was willing to act immediately, with rabid vengeance. Some scholars have speculated that Barabbas was perhaps in league with such an attitude, if not a leader. He was in prison at the time for having been involved in an insurrection that had taken place in Jerusalem probably only a few days earlier. He must have killed a Roman soldier because he was described as a murderer and was probably slated for Crucifixion on that Friday.

At the time of Christ, there was a belief that the Messiah would be, like David, a great warrior-king who would lead the Jews to a golden time that would surpass the reigns of David and Solomon. Perhaps Judas held to this ideology. Another ideology among the Jews of the time was that of the Pharisees: If the chosen people stuck to the letter of the law, God would simply elevate Israel to its former glory, the Romans would leave without a battle—or become Jews— and peace would come. A third perspective was the more common one: It didn't matter who controlled the land, they just needed to be faithful Jews. Living by the law was part of this, but faith and belief were what really mattered.

Still, no one really liked the Romans, and everyone wished they would leave. Jesus walked this middle ground; though there are occasional clues that He leaned in the direction of having a direct revolt. Judas may have taken his cues from such comments from Christ as "The Son of Man is to come with His angels in the glory of His Father, and then He will repay everyone for what they have done. Truly, I tell you, there are some standing here who will not taste death before they see the Son of Man coming in His glory" (Matthew 16:27–28).

Perhaps when Judas heard this, he felt as though he would be among those who would not taste death until after the Son of Man had come. Perhaps Judas's motive in betraying Christ was to initiate the holy battle, to get Jesus to act as the great warrior-king Judas thought He must be and to force Jesus to show His hand instead of waiting patiently for everyone to just believe. Judas may have thought of Jesus as the Messiah but not as a Savior; as king more than a healer; a leader of warriors rather than a leader of faith. Judas thought that the kingdom of Israel was more important than the kingdom of God!

Judas walked right up to Jesus and said, "Greetings, Rabbi!" And he kissed Him (26:49).

Perhaps he thought that this would be the moment Jesus would turn into a super-warrior, but all Jesus did was surrender. "Friend, do what you are here to do" (v. 50a). I think Judas would be haunted for the rest of his life by the voice of Jesus speaking the word *friend*. Only in Luke is it written that Jesus told His betrayer, "Judas, would you betray the Son of Man with a kiss?" (Luke 22:48).

A kiss is a sign of intimacy. It's an affectionate touch that expresses a very special relationship. A kiss is usually shared between people who have a very close bond. A kiss is a type of embrace that indicates not only admiration, but companionship and friendship. It is a declaration of devotion and a sweet sign of love.

But Judas used his kiss as a signal that would expose Jesus to those who sought his harm. And yet, his kiss was somehow much more than a way of pointing out, for the vigilante crowd, the man they would want to arrest. This is because there is a deep feeling evoked by Judas's act and the misuse of that kiss. Something that is generally seen as a gentle sign of intimacy was corrupted into a sign of treachery.

The story is told in such a way that we are offended when we hear it. It hurts us to feel the irony of the situation. We are repulsed by what happens. Not only is it absurd that the scribes and pharisees would bring out a gang of men with swords and clubs to capture Him, because Jesus was a teacher of peace and love and sincerity, but we're also disgusted by the irony of the insensitivity of Judas's very disrespectful use of false affection.

False affection hurts when it is exposed. It makes us feel toyed with, manipulated, used. It makes us feel betrayed. How might Jesus have felt? Judas was one of his twelve closest disciples. He had learned what Jesus had said about the kingdom of heaven. He had heard about the importance of unconditional love, true righteousness, and faith; and yet, it seems, he still did not understand. The chief priests and the elders sent out this gang of thugs to arrest Jesus, and Judas led them! Were they that threatened by this prince of peace? Perhaps they—and Judas—imagined that the messiah would be the invincible superhero, the warrior-king that some parts of the Old Testament seem to describe. And perhaps Jesus's agony at Gethsemane was so intense because He knew His simple surrender would not reveal the true meaning of the messiah.

It would not be understood. To many, surrender is a sign of weakness, not of loyalty or of determination.

The expectations of the messiah were visions of power. How would Jesus have felt? In some respects, I can't help but imagine that He felt a terrible disappointment. But He also knew that all this had to happen. Jesus was aware of the distorted understandings of what He should be and do. But His surrender proves a power far greater than that of all their vain and proud visions of power.

Sure, He could have called upon legions of angels, using the divine power granted to Him as the Son of God, to defend himself (Matthew 26:53). But that is not an expression of faith. It is little more than a flashy exhibition of power. But the power of true faith is known in surrender. Anyone can fight, but power doesn't prove the kingdom of heaven. The kingdom of heaven comes to those who surrender their lives to God, to Christ, to the movement of His Spirit.

At Gethsemane, there is a brief burst of destructive violence that virtually amounts to nothing. Apparently, one of the disciples had a sword and wielded it impulsively to inflict the minor injury of cutting off the ear of the high priest's slave. I get the impression that the disciple got the immediate feeling that this was a senseless thing to do. It was futile. There would have welled up an immediate sensation, a sudden discovery or rediscovery that "this is not what we're all about." You can't defend discipleship with violence. You can't defend it with anger or by fighting. Nor by false affections. "Then all of the disciples deserted Him and fled" (v. 56b).

Rather than doing the faithful thing, taking the risk of surrendering with Jesus, they all betrayed their loyalty. How have you betrayed your loyalties? Who do you know who has betrayed their loyalties to you, to Christ, or to the church? Where are his or her affections? And for the disciples, where was their love for their master? At a time when their greatest need for faith was indicated, they all deserted.

This story is *our* story. Each one of us has displayed false affections at one time or another in our spiritual journeys. We may say we love Christ, and yet we betray our loyalty to Him. Our loyalty often hinges either on our feelings of well-being, and we want to boost our egos another cubit, or it hinges on our woundedness and our desires for a quick cure. For many, it's either bandwagon faith or Band-Aid faith. We climb aboard because we feel like it will serve our best interests, or we come looking for healing, not realizing that most of the time, our wounds never would have occurred if we had been faithful in the first place.

Seldom do we realize our betrayal of Christ!

"Jesus has many lovers of his kingdom, but few bearers of his cross. Jesus has many who desire his consolation; but few are willing to partake in his tribulation. Jesus has many who follow him to the receiving of the blessed bread of life; but few will follow him in the drinking of the cup of passion" (Thomas à Kempis, *Imitation of Christ*). Add to this: How gladly we go in search for salvation; how poorly we rise to serve in His mission. How quickly we come forward to receive His forgiveness; how slowly we move to forgive one another. How glorious it is to be filled by His love; how shameful our witness to His spirit of sacrifice. How wonderful it is to be rich with His blessings; how poor we must be when we keep them unshared. How great it is to be healed by His grace; how ungracious we are when we are uncaring. How much we will long for the joy of His justice; how easy it is to forget that He's our judge. How easy it is to cherish His peace; how feeble our efforts are to partake in His pain.

How wonderful it is to be inspired by His calling to be His disciples; how humbling it is when His calling is betrayed. Heaven help us!

However it all happened, Jesus was arrested. A very brief scuttle ensued, but Jesus put an immediate stop to it, saying, "All who take up the sword will die by the sword" (26:52). The implication is that you reap what you sow. Bloodshed only leads to more bloodshed. But then, Jesus says something rather wonderful and curious at the same time. It is wonderful when you think of how glorious it would be, and it is curious in that it was not done: "Don't you know that I can appeal to My Father, and He will at once send me more than twelve legions of angels?" (v. 53). Power! But it is unused.

That would be awesome! Wow! But what would faith in Christ be if that had happened? Would we really have faith, or would we be the same as the zealots—with great expectations but minimal faith. Maybe that's about where Christian culture is these days. Our expectations of ourselves have little to do with spiritual growth and encouraging others to grow, but a lot to do with what Jesus can and has done for us as individuals—and what He will do for us in the sweet by and by.

But Jesus explains that what is happening is fulfilling the scriptures (vv. 54 and 56a). More on that later. At this moment, as the climax unfolds, Jesus takes a final jab at the chief priests and elders. "Have you come out with swords and clubs to arrest me as though I was a bandit?" (26:55). They only did this under a blanket of darkness because "they feared the crowds, because they regarded Jesus as a prophet" (Matthew 21:46). They could have arrested Jesus anytime. "Day after day, I sat in the Temple teaching, and you did not arrest Me" (26:55b).

How deceitful you are, chief priests and elders! They would never do anything that would expose themselves as obvious hypocrites or that would cause them to lose favor before the people. They had no favor with the people anyway, but they had their power. Jesus's comment reveals their character to them as so blatantly against Jesus that, later, no one would have any respect for them. They held their status only before the people because they were puppets of Rome, and Rome backed them up.

Again, Jesus tells those who could hear Him that "All this has taken place so that the Scriptures of the prophets may be fulfilled" (v. 56a). Surrender, surrender, surrender. Then all the disciples deserted Him and fled.

Then Jesus was more alone than ever. No one could go through it with Him, and no one should go through life without Him.at

The Trial

Those who had arrested Jesus
took him to Caiaphas the high priest,
in whose house the scribes and elders gathered.
But Peter was following him at a distance,
as far as the courtyard of the high priest;
and going inside, he sat with the guards
in order to see how this would end.
Now the chief priests and the whole council
were looking for false testimony against Jesus
so that they might put him to death,
but they found none, though many false witnesses came forward.
At last two came forward and said,
"This fellow said,
'I am able to destroy the temple of God
and to build it in three days.'"
The high priest stood up and said,
"Have you no answer? What is it they testify against you?"
But Jesus was silent.
Then the high priest said to him,
"I put you under oath before the living God,
tell us if you are the Messiah, the Son of God."
Jesus said to him,
"You have said so.
But I tell you,

From now on you will see the Son of Man
seated at the right hand of Power
and coming on the clouds of heaven."
Then the high priest tore his clothes and said,
"He has blasphemed! Why do we still need witnesses?
You have heard his blasphemy. What is your verdict?"
They answered,
"He deserves death."
Then they spat in his face, and struck him, and some slapped him,
saying, "Prophesy to us, you Messiah! Who is it that struck you?"
(Matthew 26:57–68)

They didn't care about anyone but Jesus. The disciples had all deserted Him, but Peter must have run only so far. He stayed out of view, away from the torchlight, quietly "following at a distance" in the darkness (v. 58). We know it was Peter who had brandished a sword and cut off the ear of the first servant of the high priest. We know this because John tells us so in his gospel (John 18:10). We even learn there that the servant's name was Malchus. This violent act should have gotten Peter arrested, but as I said, they were only concerned with Jesus.

They were taking Him to the house of Caiaphas, the high priest. The elders had gathered in order to deal with Jesus. Apparently, they were all in on the conspiracy to arrest Jesus and bring Him to trial through the course of the night, during the hours of darkness, where evil lurks about. In the gospel of John, John reports Jesus saying, "This is the Judgment—that the light has come into the world, and people loved darkness rather than light because their deeds were evil. For all who do evil hate the light and do not come to the light, so that their deeds may not be exposed" (John 3:19–20).

But the story of the trial exposed them. Peter lingered in the shadows, virtually unseen. After a while, he would be noticed, but initially, he was simply a spectator. Matthew reports that he sat near the guards, "in order to see how this would end" (v. 58b). It's easy to wonder what Peter expected. Many scholars assume he may have held the belief (at least partially, wishing it would be true) that the

Messiah would become a great warrior-king, and perhaps at any time, the twelve legions of angels that Jesus mentioned back in verse fifty-three would come to the rescue. But they never came. Jesus never summoned them.

Caiaphas's house was probably very similar to any house of a wealthy family of the day. There was the original building, where the patriarch probably lived. We know that person to have been Annas, the father-in-law of Caiaphas. As the family grew and the adult children married, they would build an addition, a connected home, architecturally "attached" to the first. Often, there were other family members whose homes were likewise attached, and a rectangular courtyard would eventually take shape in the center. It is not unlikely that a large room or "great hall" would be part of the floor plan where everyone would gather to eat. This was where the Sanhedrin gathered seventy elders. It is probable that they all had to stand because there were not enough chairs for everyone. The courtyard must have overlooked the space of this great room—which would have been out of view from the street. Because Caiaphas was a public figure, people would have had access to the courtyard, so Peter was able to sneak in and blend in. The courtyard would have had several servants of the elders watching in wait as the trial went on.

Matthew's perspective of the trial is blatantly present as he tells the story: "Now the chief priests and the whole council were looking for *false* testimony against Jesus so that they might put him to death, but they found none, though many false witnesses came forward" (vv. 59–60). Of course, it was against the law to offer false witness, commandment number nine (Exodus 20:16), so you can see how deeply in league with the darkness they had become. Through it all, Jesus was silent (v. 63).

Finally, two witnesses testified to the same thing, which automatically made it "true." They reported that Jesus had said, "I am able to destroy this Temple of God and to build it in three days" (Matthew 26:61). What He actually said was in response to a request from the Jewish leaders for a sign to give legitimacy for His having cleansed the Temple courts of the moneychangers. Referring to His own body, Jesus said, "Destroy *this* Temple, and in three days I will raise it up" (John 2:18–19). However, His words were misconstrued, and it offended the best interests of the Sanhedrin. Still, "Jesus was silent" (v. 63).

In the gospel of Mark, when Jesus was silent, one of the accusers said, "Have you no answer to make?" (14:60). Still, however, he was silent. And there, in that silence, Peter could have rushed in and testified what he had proclaimed long ago: "You are the Christ, the Son of the living God" (Matthew 16:16). But there was just silence. I wonder how long it lasted. But I want to say that there, in that sort of silence, is our summons. The silence of Christ comes when defending Himself would have been crucial; when defending Him, *we* are crucial. It is our time. We are His witnesses. When Jesus is silent, *we* need to speak. When Jesus says nothing on His own behalf, it is our turn to answer—His disciples, if we *are* His disciples!

Jesus is often silent in our world. But He is waiting. For too many people, Jesus is silent. His silence is manifested even in some of the people in our own families. They suffer trials (sometimes even silently), and Jesus is silent. Some of those trials may be brought on by circumstances of their own choosing, but why is Christ silent in their lives? Why should He seem to be almost absent? Perhaps it is because He is given no voice. How could He speak, if not through you or me? Jesus is so silent today because we are not speaking up. And for those who are waiting for Jesus to speak in their lives, if we do not answer to His summons, the next time they hear Jesus speak might be as their judge! "You will see the Son of Man seated at the right hand of power, and coming with the clouds of heaven" (Mark 16:62).

At His trial, Jesus gave no answer at first. That ticked them off. Caiaphas railed: "I put you under oath before the living God, tell us if you are the Messiah, the son of God" (v. 63b). So Jesus nailed it down. "You have said so. But I tell you, from now on you will see the Son of Man seated at the right hand of power, coming on the clouds of heaven" (v. 64).

Daniel had this vision: "As I watched in the night visions, I saw one like a Son of Man coming with the clouds of heaven. And He came to the Ancient of Days and was presented before Him. To Him was given dominion and glory and kingship, that all peoples, nations, and languages should serve Him. His dominion is an everlasting dominion that shall not pass away and His kingship is one that shall never be destroyed" (Daniel 7:7–13).

Jesus was claiming this vision for Himself. I imagine Peter's heart was beginning to race as he looked for the legions of angels to come right then. When I read this story, I want to put a hushed pause and a great gasp in the Sanhedrin as they heard this. Did they fear the idea that twelve legions of angels might appear at any moment? But when nothing happened, the cry of "Blasphemy!" rose up.

Blasphemy happens when someone claims to be God or claims something or someone to be God that is not actually God. It could also happen by saying something about God that just is not true. It's usually so obvious that there is no mistake about it; it is blasphemy, plain and simple. And yet, we live in a time when new-age gurus and quasi-Christian speakers are compelling people to claim their own "god-hoods," their own divinities, their "true" natures. Blasphemy is all around us, and we barely notice it. It's in the idolatry that puts first anything that is not God. God should be first in all things.

Friends, *we* are on trial today. Christianity is on trial. The church is on trial. Her witnesses lack integrity. Christianity lacks relevance, and we have watered down the truth. We need to rise up to meet the challenge of these days. Don't ignore it. The church is still the body of Christ to the world. And yet we are weak before the powers of secularism, of worldliness, and of decadence. What is the verdict on the church? It is irrelevant to an irreverent world.

The world is saying with the elders, "He deserves death" (v. 66). And like the false phonies they were, "they spat in His face and struck Him," and slapped Him around (v. 67). And today, His body, the church, is being slapped by the superficiality of those who claim faith so nominally. It is spit on with the words *irrelevant* and *hypocrite.* And what seems to strike us the hardest is the indifference of the world to Jesus.

Rise up! Rise up in hope! Believe that "from now on you will see the son of Man seated at the right hand of power, coming on the clouds" (v. 64).

Rise up and look. Raise your expectations. Work for the kingdom, and pray for the kingdom to come!

The Denial

Now Peter was sitting outside in the courtyard.
A servant-girl came to him and said,
"You also were with Jesus the Galilean."
But he denied it before all of them, saying,
"I do not know what you ae talking about."
When he went out to the porch, another servant-girl saw him,
and she said to the bystanders,
"This man was with Jesus of Nazareth."
Again he denied it with an oath, "I do not know the man."
After a little while the bystanders came up
and said to Peter,
"Certainly you are also one of them, for your accent betrays you."
Then he began to curse, and he swore an oath,
"I do not know the man!"
At that moment the cock crowed.
Then Peter remembered what Jesus had said:
"Before the cock crows, you will deny me three times."
And he went out and wept bitterly.
(Matthew 26:69–75)

Peter's heart was sinking as he watched the elders of the Sanhedrin slapping Jesus, spitting on Him, and mocking Him. This was his Lord! Peter believed Jesus was "the Christ, the Son of the Living God!" He said so before all the disciples at Caesarea Philippi when Jesus asked, "Who do you say that I am?" (Matthew 16:15–16). No legions of angels were coming to the rescue. All the other disciples had deserted Jesus. Racing through his mind was all the ways he should come to Jesus's defense and rescue, but he was full of fear, and he was only one man. There were guards standing close by, watching what was happening as well. Could Peter summon the angels? He probably wished he could. He felt so helpless. It hurt to see Jesus treated so poorly. And it should cut into us, too, that Jesus was treated this way. Yet this was only the beginning. They had said that Jesus "deserved death" (Matthew 26:66).

To add insult to injury, Peter was no longer able to go unnoticed. At least one person was aware of him. "A servant-girl came to him and said, 'You also were with Jesus the Galilean'" (v. 69). What was on her mind? Was she trying to get Peter in trouble? Guilt by association? Was she appealing for him to do something? Was she sympathetic to Jesus and His followers? Did she want Peter to know that she felt his pain, or was she just being antagonistic? "He denied it before all of them ..." Apparently, "all of them" were observing Peter now. He couldn't hide. Maybe he was afraid of "all of them," not just the guards. He looked around, his eyes darting. Everyone was looking at *him*. "He denied it before all of them," not just the servant girl, "'I do not know what you are talking about!'" (v. 70).

He was trying to tell her not to bother him. But "all of them" must have wondered about him. Why was he there? What was he waiting for? Who was he? The servants in the house of Caiaphas probably knew who the servants of the elders were. They could recognize who the guards were. If there were others who were curious about a trial that was happening after midnight, who came into the courtyard just to watch, they probably would have been some of the Jerusalem night people, and they could probably be easily distinguished in some way. But here was one man, unconnected to any of them, who was sober, not a servant, not a guard, not a political observer, a Jew, a tradesman by his clothes, not wealthy—but he was watching. Who was he?

Peter moved away from the crowd. "He went out to the porch" (v. 71a). Could he still see Jesus? He couldn't bear to watch what they were doing to Him. And Jesus just took it! Peter's heart probably sank lower and lower. He had just lied ... to save himself? To claim no responsibility? He was finally, completely deserting Jesus.

But "another servant-girl saw him, and said to those standing by, 'This man *was* with Jesus of Nazareth!'" (v. 71b). Exposed! Hoping to avoid their scrutiny, Peter may have wished they would just begin to think that maybe he only looked like someone who had been with Jesus. Well, yeah! He is someone who had been with Jesus. "Again he denied it with an oath ..." (v. 72a). Implied, though not put on the lips of Peter by Matthew, are the words, "I swear ... I do not know the man" (v. 72b).

Obviously, the only people who could possibly deny Jesus are those who don't really know Him. But Peter had made his beautiful profession of faith, "You are the Christ, the Son of the Living God" (Matthew 16:16). Had he just been saying what he thought was the right thing to say, but didn't really believe it? Many do that. It happens when people make vows. It happens when people are being interviewed for jobs. It happens when people run for political office. But when Peter said that Jesus was "the Christ, the Son of the Living God," Jesus responded by telling all the disciples, "Flesh and blood has not revealed this to you, but My Father in heaven. And I tell you, [speaking directly to Peter], you are Peter (*petros*), and on this rock (*petra*), [the rock of Peter's words] I will build my Church" (Matthew 16:17–18). As long as the Spirit of Christ, the Son of the living God, is vital in a church, nothing can prevail against it. The church is the body of Christ as long as Christ is the head and as long as Jesus is professed as the Christ, the Son of the living God! And the worst of the worst, "the gates of Hades shall not prevail against it" (16:18).

But that's where Peter was feeling himself to be. Several of those who had been standing by were now watching Peter's first trial! He would have other trials, and he would endure much for the sake of the faith, but for now, Peter was on trial. They "came up and said to Peter, "Certainly you are also one of them." (v. 73a). "*One of them!*" Have you ever been categorized as "one of *them?*" It sets you apart from "the rest of *us.*"

"Your accent betrays you" (v. 73b). You could recognize someone from Galilee as easily as you might recognize someone from *Chicaaago*. And if this man in the courtyard was from Galilee, they presumed he must have some affiliation with Jesus, the man from Galilee. The teacher who had disciples and followers, who had healed, who had confronted the chief priests and the elders, who had ridden into Jerusalem only days before as the people regaled Him with Hosannas and proclaimed Him to be "blessed, the one who comes in the name of the Lord" (Matthew 21:9).

Had Peter forgotten it all? Was he feeling disillusioned? Disappointed? Discouraged? Why didn't Jesus call on the angelic legions to come to His aid? Every question racing through his mind was like a hammer's blow against Satan's chisel, poised upon the rock-solidness that was Peter's faith. Peter was turning into sand, and at that moment, he was just falling apart. "He began to curse ... he swore an oath, 'I do not know the man!'" (v. 74a).

The cock crowed! Even before Peter finished his sentence, "At that moment the cock crowed" (v. 74b). Immediately, Peter was flooded with such an immense awareness of his lie that grief welled up inside him. He couldn't hold back the tears. He "remembered what Jesus had said," back in verse thirty-four: "Before the cock crows, you will deny me three times" (v. 75). At this moment of Peter's deepest darkness, a sharp light pierced through right to his heart. Jesus knew! How could He have known unless the Spirit of the living God was in Him? There was no question, Jesus is the Christ. What was happening to Him was fulfilling the scriptures. "Like a lamb that is led to the slaughter, and like a sheep that before its shearers is silent, so He did not open His mouth" (Isaiah 53:7).

Realization had cut through Peter's fear, and as he became more and more aware of Jesus as the Messiah in that moment, he came face-to-face with the fact that he had just denied Him three times. He couldn't escape the truth. He couldn't escape his failure, but he could escape the courtyard. "And he went out and wept bitterly" (v. 75).

Peter couldn't help but condemn himself. His master was being condemned to death, slapped, punched, and spit on. Things would get worse for Jesus—much worse. Peter walked away, lost, empty, and deeply disappointed in himself. His heart was broken. But "a broken and contrite heart, God will not despise" (Psalm 51:17).

Denial is a bitter thing. Very bitter. Reversing it is hard. But that's exactly what Peter would do. He would join the others. They had deserted Jesus, but none of them had done so as seriously as he just had. Peter was going to find a way to overcome his failure, if at least he could encourage the others. Because he knew Jesus was the Christ, he knew that this wasn't over yet. Peter may not have known yet how it would continue, but he would overcome. And he would help the others overcome as well, except for one of them.

That's what's next. For now, just realize that there is a way to overcome the failures we suffer. There is always a way. Judas couldn't imagine it. Peter could.

The Remorse

When morning came,
all the chief priests and the elders of the people
conferred together against Jesus
in order to bring about his death.
They bound him, and led him away,
and handed him over to Pilate the governor.
When Judas, his betrayer,
saw that Jesus was condemned,
he repented
and brought back the thirty pieces of silver
to the chief priests and the elders.
He said, "I have sinned by betraying innocent blood."
But they said, "What is that to us? See to it yourself."
Throwing down the pieces of silver in the temple,
he departed;
and he went and hanged himself.
But the chief priests, taking the pieces of silver, said,
"It is not lawful to put them into the treasury,
since they are blood money."
After conferring together,
they used them to buy the potter's field
as a place to bury foreigners.
For this reason that field has been called
the Field of Blood to this day.

Then was fulfilled what had been spoken
through the prophet Jeremiah,
"And they took the thirty pieces of silver,
the price of one on whom a price had been set,
on whom some of the people of Israel had set a price,
and they gave them for the potter's field,
as the Lord commanded me."
(Matthew 27:1–10)

Peter was weeping. Stumbling toward … what? He was going to find the others, the ones who had run away. Where could they be? Would they have regrouped back at the Mount of Olives? We know they got together again, at least by Sunday morning. I imagine that none of them had slept since Jesus was arrested. They probably felt afraid for their lives! Some may have fled together in the same direction. Maybe it would have been safest if they all separated. But sometimes, you just need to be with a few familiar faces, a friendly presence, when a crisis occurs. Some have suggested that they all eventually rallied together at the home of Lazarus, Mary, and Martha. That's in Bethany, a short walk from Gethsemane. Others have suggested that Lazarus owned the olive grove on the Mount of Olives. Whatever and however things happened, they eventually regrouped, though at least by the afternoon, John had gone to the site of the Crucifixion, according to his gospel. Meanwhile, Jesus was being taken to Pontius Pilate. They, the chief priests and the elders, "conferred together against Jesus in order to bring about His death" (27:1). They were bound and determined to silence Jesus, primarily because He had revealed their falsehood, exposed their hypocrisy, and uncovered their error!

The disciples, however, all regrouped except for one: Judas. The sun would soon begin to rise. The darkness would disburse. People would begin to see more clearly soon, or would they? Maybe there was a bit of a haze beginning to rise. Judas felt as if he'd made a huge mistake. Judas may have been nearby, watching the trial too. If he was, he did a better job than Peter of going unnoticed. Somehow, he was aware that Jesus had been condemned. Did he know that Jesus said almost nothing during His trial? Did Judas expect to see Jesus appeal for the angels to come, a warrior-spirit to rise in Jesus, and a battle to begin? And then when it didn't, he might have felt as if he'd betrayed Jesus to death, rather than incite the Messiah to take control and wield His power, to rise to victory.

"He repented" (v. 3). Judas knew he was wrong. He wanted to turn things around. Because there had been a conspiracy and Judas was embroiled in the center of it, he went back to the main conspirators. Not many went with the guards as Jesus was taken to Pilate, so the Sanhedrin was still informally gathered. Several—probably most of them, actually—went to the Temple. It was the day of Passover, the holiest of days to the Jews. They had to prepare. That's where Judas went. That's where forgiveness and reconciliation could be found: in the Temple.

He "brought back the thirty pieces of silver to the Chief Priests and the Elders" (v. 3b). He was contrite and full of remorse. He confessed: "I have sinned by betraying innocent blood" (v. 4a). In Deuteronomy 27:24, it says, "Cursed be anyone who takes a bribe to shed innocent blood." Maybe Judas knew that what he did was an accursed thing. The chief priests and the elders were part of it. They paid the bribe. They were sinners by association in the conspiracy. *They* had done an accursed thing too. But they were also the only ones who could absolve Judas. Instead, they said, "What is that to us? See to it yourself'" (v. 4b). Rather than prescribe any form of penance, rather than express any compassion, rather than do the kindest part of their job, these religious leaders were cold and harsh. Judas was just a tool to them. They didn't care about him. He'd served his purpose. They could have discarded trash less carelessly.

Judas saw their nature, their dark hearts, their puny resentment of his rabbi. Judas believed in Jesus. But his belief was distorted by his twisted expectations. Maybe he knew this now. But he also knew that all the chief priests and the elders cared about was getting Jesus out of the way. Judas may never have realized that anything he did was fulfilling prophecy, and, very obviously, neither did these religious leaders.

Anger was welling up inside of Judas. His coconspirators were turning their backs on him. He threw down the thirty pieces of silver to the Temple floor and left (v. 5). Where could he go? His fellow disciples knew what he'd done. He began to hate himself. He had betrayed Jesus. He had been rejected by the chief priests and elders. He was lost. Self-loathing was churning away in his mind. Like Peter, his heart was broken, but Judas had had a role in breaking Jesus's heart. The thought couldn't get out of his mind. Like a hot, sharp knife stabbing into his brain, he couldn't escape himself.

Meanwhile, Jesus was being taken before Pilate. The chief priests and elders at the Temple began a casual conversation about what to do with the thirty pieces of silver. How was their discussion made known to Matthew? Could it have been overheard by a Temple servant who, after the Resurrection—maybe even after the Day of Pentecost—shared it with the disciples? Could it have come from one of the elders who later became a believer? Some people do realize that there are mistakes they have made and try to overcome them, especially when they finally see the light.

But these chief priests and elders admitted among themselves that the thirty pieces of silver were "blood money." It couldn't go into the Temple treasury. They decided to put the money to a good cause to, what, ...assuage their own guilt? They would buy (after the Passover) a "potter's field as a place to bury foreigners" (v. 7). More likely, it was a place to bury slaves. Thirty shekels of silver was the price of a slave (Exodus 21:32).

By now, the day of Passover was beginning to be filled with activity. Lambs were being brought to the Temple, families were gathering together, Jesus was standing before Pilate, and Judas tied a rope around his neck to hang himself (Matthew 27:5b). His remorse had dug into his heart like a dull nail. His self-loathing made him think that this was his only escape. He felt as if he could never rise above the guilt of his betrayal. Any light in his life was only further exposing the darkness of his deed. Echoing in his mind were likely the last words Jesus had said to him: "Friend, do what you are here to do" (26:50). *Friend*? Judas failed as a friend. He could see no way forward. He felt only torment. Maybe he even felt as though he didn't deserve to live. His death would be his entrance into eternal torment, maybe. Judas *had* repented. He *had* confessed his sin. Could he leave the world a sign of his remorse, of his contrition? Could his death tell others not to do what he had done? Or is Judas only a pathetic pawn that served a plan greater than he ever knew? (And if so, why would God do this to someone?)

I think the world needs this sign of remorse, and the message of the wrongness of betrayal. But will the world get the whole message? The message of Peter's life? The message that you can rise above the denials and shortcomings we experience and take on the blessing of forgiveness—the healing that is the Resurrection, the power that is the spirit of faith? If you ever feel remorse for your sins, the answer is never suicide. We all need to seek the Lord while He may be found!

I pity Judas. Not because I like him or admire him, but because he is just so pitiful. Might he be included in Jesus first prayer from the cross: "Father, forgive them for they know not what they do?" (Luke 23:34).

Heaven help us all!

The Governor

Now Jesus stood before the governor;
and the governor asked him, "Are you the King of the Jews?"
Jesus said, "You say so."
But when he was accused by the chief priests and elders,
he did not answer. Then Pilate said to him,
"Do you not hear how many accusations they make against you?"
But he gave him no answer, not even to a single charge,
so that the governor was greatly amazed.
Now at the festival
the governor was accustomed to release a prisoner for the crowd,
anyone whom they wanted.
At that time they had a notorious prisoner called Jesus Barabbas.
So after they had gathered,
Pilate said to them, "Whom do you want me to release for you,
Jesus Barabbas or Jesus who is called the Messiah?"
For he realized that it was out of jealousy
that they had handed him over.
While he was sitting on the judgment seat,
his wife sent word to him,
"Have nothing to do with that innocent man,
for today I have suffered a great deal
because of a dream about him."
Now the chief priests and the elders persuaded the crowd
to ask for Barabbas and have Jesus killed.
The governor again said to them,

"Which of the two do you want me to release for you?"
And they said, "Barabbas."
Pilate said to them,
"Then what should I do with Jesus who is called the Messiah?"
All of them said,
"Let him be crucified!"
Then he asked, "Why, what evil has he done?"
But they shouted all the more, "Let him be crucified!"
So when Pilate saw that he could do nothing,
but rather that a riot was beginning,
he took some water and washed his hands before the crowd,
saying, "I am innocent of this man's blood;
see to it yourselves."
Then the people as a whole answered,
"His blood be upon us and on our children!"
So he released Barabbas for them;
and after flogging Jesus, he handed him over to be crucified.
(Matthew 27:11–26)

Pilate may not have been the best diplomat, but he was able to see through the falseness of the chief priests and the elders who brought Jesus before him. He saw their character well enough for it to have become an historical statement that, concerning Jesus, "he realized that it was out of jealousy that they had handed Him over" (27:18). He realized that Jesus was just a pawn in their power games. Pilate must have heard enough about Jesus to know that He was very popular. It is very likely that he had heard about Jesus's healing work. Maybe he had even heard about some of what Jesus had taught.

Likewise, Pilate's wife was conscious of who Jesus was. Or at least, she was aware of what others said about Jesus. The Palm Sunday triumphal entry into Jerusalem would not have gone unnoticed by the powers that be. There may have been some serious speculation about Jesus as well as about Barabbas in the governor's court. A primary assumption about Pilate is that his number-one purpose was to rein in any irritating troubles, any discontent, and any activities that might have been a threat to the Pax Romana—the Roman peace. Even though it was peace under oppression and order under tyranny, it was unholy to the Jews because the Romans were pagan idol-worshipers. Theirs was the power of conquest and control by threat of crucifixion. They were hated by the Jews for all of this, not to mention the burdensome Roman taxes.

King Herod was a puppet king. The high priest secured his position by purchasing it from the Roman governor, and Roman troops in every town were tolerated only at the threat of severe punishment. And here, in this episode subsequent to Jesus's Crucifixion, the Jewish leaders concern themselves with Pilate only to get him to order Jesus's execution.

Pilate's first question to Jesus had to do with the issue of power. "Are you the king of the Jews?" (Matthew 27:11). In other words, are you guilty of sedition against the empire? Again, the question states the fact. He wouldn't have asked if it couldn't be true. Jesus said, "You have said so" (Matthew 26:64). This was the same way He had responded to Caiaphas when he demanded to know if Jesus was the Messiah (Matthew 26:63).

The Jewish leaders began to enumerate their accusations, but Jesus was again silent. Pilate wondered at Jesus's lack of defense against their charges. He was probably used to seeing people squirm, especially before the threat of being crucified. Pilate couldn't understand the posture of one surrendered to a purpose greater than this life, greater than this world. We, too, need to be surrendered to our purpose in Christ.

Pilate saw the absurdity of these Jewish leaders in their determination to have Jesus done away with. He gave them an option. It was actually an extremely poor attempt at diplomacy. Barabbas was, without a doubt, a criminal. Pilate would release Jesus in order to preserve His life, because he didn't think Jesus was a real threat to the empire. At best, he might have thought Him to be delusional. Barabbas, on the other hand, was an actual threat. Even Pilate's wife sensed Jesus's innocence. She may only have had a dream that told her so, and it caused her some serious anguish, but she appealed to Pilate through a messenger to "have nothing to do with that innocent man" (v. 19).

Too late. Meanwhile, some of "the chief priests and elders persuaded the crowds to ask for Barabbas and to have Jesus killed" (v. 20). The crowds were gathering, not at the court of the governor, but on their way to the courts of the Temple, not far from where Pilate would ask for their decision. The praetorium, Pilate's headquarters, was his official residence in Jerusalem. Scholars locate it in the western corner of the city wall, not far from the Temple. But many people were on their way there for worship, and the worship experience would have lasted a better part of the day.

Pilate sat on a "bench at the place called the Stone Pavement" (John 19:13), where he would pronounce judgment. This spot overlooked a sort of plaza where many people could gather. "The Governor again said to them, 'Which of the two do you want me to release for you?' And they said, 'Barabbas.' Pilate then said to them, 'Then what should I do with Jesus who is called the Christ?' All of them said, 'Let Him be crucified!'" (vv. 21–22). *All of them?* Had the chief priests and elders done such a good job at convincing the people to "ask for Barabbas and have Jesus killed" (v. 20)? Were they that complicit with the Jewish leaders, or were they confused? Were they really even aware of what was going on? Did they see in Pilate's question an example of generous magnanimity? What happened? Didn't they realize that this was Jesus, whom the crowds—probably very different people by now—had recently welcomed into Jerusalem with palm branches and Hosannas?

Scholars have suggested that, yes, it was a different crowd. Those gathering there were more likely to have been more recently arrived pilgrims not from Jerusalem or its environs, as was more likely the case on Palm Sunday, but rather from a greater distance away. Perhaps they were even from different countries, some of them, and their languages were different. The sound of the name *Barabbas* might indicate to them the "son of the father." These people may not have felt the hypocrisy of the Jewish leaders as much as the locals had, so they might have been more easily persuaded by these "leaders." Either way, this needed to happen to fulfill the prophecies about Christ and the purpose of redemption. "Let Him be crucified" (v. 22).

But then Pilate asked the best question of all: "Why, what evil has he done?" (v. 23). Yes! What evil? Certainly, from Pilate's point of view, nothing deserving death. But there was no answer. "They shouted all the more, 'Let Him be crucified!'" (v. 23b).

"So when Pilate saw that he could do nothing ..." (v. 24a). What? Pilate was the one in control, wasn't he? No. God was. Pilate had, in effect, generated a riot. But to show contempt, he ritualistically washed his hands of the whole thing and said, "I am innocent of this man's blood. See to it yourselves" (v. 24). "See to it yourselves"? Isn't that what the Jewish leaders had said to Judas? "See to it yourself" (27:4).

I'm not responsible, he's saying, *you* are. "Then the people, as a whole, answered, 'His blood be on us and on our children!'" (v. 25). In other words, "You're relieved of the matter. You don't have to answer for this execution. We will."

Ultimately, it was God's plan that Jesus would suffer for humanity's guilt and die for humanity's sin. But as much as Judas was only a tool for the chief priests and the elders in the arrest of Jesus, so were the chief priests and the elders only a tool for God in bringing about Jesus's execution.

We are all tools being used by God to bring about His purposes. We are the instruments of a divine purpose. We are here to serve God's design. Or, if not, we will serve either our own purposes, or Satan's. But the difference will be made by our legacy, which can be how we—or those who might reflect on the legacy of our lives—will answer Pilate's most relevant question: What evil have *you* done?

Pilate released Barabbas for them, and then, just to reclaim some control of the situation, he had Jesus flogged. Finally, he gave them what they wanted. He handed Jesus over to be crucified (v. 26). But that's what we all should want. We need a Savior. We may not want to think about how Jesus was crucified or about *how* we are saved, but His death is what saves us. It had to happen in the world. So it happened in a very worldly way, with very human instruments and very horrible experiences. But as we accept it, it makes a difference in our lives. We are saved!

The Pavement

So when Pilate saw that he could do nothing,
but rather that a riot was beginning,
he took some water and washed his hands before the crowd, saying,
"I am innocent of this man's blood; see to it yourselves."
Then the people as a whole answered,
"His blood be on us and on our children!"
So he released Barabbas for them;
and after flogging Jesus, he handed him over to be crucified.
(Matthew 27:24–26)

Meditating through the gospel of Matthew, I began on the Mount of Olives, where there was an olive orchard and an oil press, a *gethsemane*. There, Jesus gathered with all his disciples, except for one. And nearby, He prayed, "Father, if it is possible, may this cup be taken from me. Yet, not as I will, but as You will" (26:39). Jesus was "overwhelmed with sorrow," and He asked Peter, James, and John to "keep watch with me" (v. 38).

While Jesus faced His deepest anguish, Judas had gone off to betray Him by leading the chief priests and elders and the temple guards to His location. Peter, James, and John fell asleep. Though they tried to keep vigil for Christ's sake, the spirit was willing, but the flesh was weak (Matthew 26:41).

After a few more hours of prayer, Jesus was arrested. "A large crowd came into the scene with swords and clubs … from the chief priests and the elders of the people" (26:47) …and Judas Iscariot. Jesus told him, "Friend, do what you are here to do" (v. 50a). There was a very brief scuffle, but Jesus put an immediate stop to it, saying, "All who take up the sword will die by the sword" (v. 52). "Then all the disciples deserted Him and fled" (26:56).

Peter followed at a distance (v. 58), and Jesus was dragged to the courtyard at the home of Caiaphas. Standing before the whole Sanhedrin (v. 59), they held a mockery of a trial. Peter watched from the shadows. They wanted to condemn Jesus, but they wanted to do it legally. It was a farce.

Meanwhile, Peter was recognized. Some thought he was one of the people who knew Jesus. He denied it three times. Jesus had told him, even before they got to the Mount of Olives, "Before the rooster crows, you will deny me three times" (26:34). When he heard the sound of the rooster, Peter was shocked into an awareness that cut so deep, he hurried away from the courtyard of Caiaphas and "wept bitterly" (26:75).

The sun had begun to rise. The remorse in Peter's heart was matched by the remorse in Judas's soul. Peter would overcome his, but Judas could not. Jesus had been bound and led away to Pilate. The scene changes to the Temple court. Judas caught up with some of the chief priests and elders there, and tried to return the thirty pieces of silver they had given him to betray his Rabbi. They didn't care. Judas was only a tool to them. They had accomplished what they wanted with him, and now he could be tossed aside. Judas was so remorseful that he went off and hanged himself (27:5).

The story of this chapter in Christ's life is so full of tragedy that it is easier to avoid than to reflect on, especially because we know how, ultimately, the story ends. But it gets worse before it gets better, and it is worth our consideration because it not only inspires us to deepen our faith, but it makes us face all the ways we are like the characters in the story.

The sun had barely risen when Pilate was aroused to duty. The scene changes to "the place called the Pavement" (John 19:13). Pilate may not have been the best diplomat, but he was able to see through the chief priests and elders who brought Jesus before him for judgment. "He realized that it was out of jealousy that they had handed Him over" (27:18). Even his wife tried to warn him to "have nothing to do with that innocent man" (v. 19). Because it was a custom, supposedly, for the governor to release one prisoner during the Passover feast, Pilate asked the gathering crowd, "'Which one do you want me to release to you: Barabbas or Jesus, who is called Christ?' For he knew that it was out of envy that they had handed Jesus over to him" (vv. 17–18). The chief priests and elders had persuaded the crowd to ask for Barabbas. Pilate, then, in a demonstration of both disdainful contempt for the Jewish leaders and a renunciation of responsibility for the judgment of Jesus, released Barabbas and, after having Jesus flogged, handed Him over to be crucified (v. 26).

That was where we left off. The scene was the Pavement. And there was the whipping post. Jesus was chained to it and flogged to within a few inches of His life. Next, Jesus was taken into the Praetorium where He was mocked and further abused before He was made to carry His cross to Golgotha to be crucified. Now we have come to the last hours in the life of Christ. Of course, we know the true end of the story of His life. The last hours have still not yet come... even today!

But the purpose of retelling the story with the deepest of details is to make it a part of *our* stories—our faith stories.

What anguish do you face the way Jesus faced his final conflict in Gethsemane? How have you surrendered yourself to the degree that you could say with Him, "Not what I want, but what You want" (26:39)? Who keeps watch with you? Over whom do you keep vigil? And how or in what ways have you failed them, as did Peter, James, and John?

Judas betrayed Jesus. How have you betrayed our Lord? It may not be by a condemnation of Jesus in particular, but by the inadequacy of our witness or the contradictions between our beliefs and our actions. How do we sometimes desert Him the way His disciples did when Jesus was arrested? Like Peter, how have we denied the Lordship of Jesus in our lives? And how have we experienced remorse for our failings? And, like Peter, how will we overcome?

Like Judas, how are we tools used by Satan to undermine what is good and graceful in this world? Like the chief priests and the elders, how is God using us to fulfill His purposes? How are we, sometimes, like Pilate, as we, like him, wash our hands of any responsibility for true justice?

Put yourself into the scenes of Christ's final conflict and His last hours. Even as a spectator, how do you feel as you observe the events that led up to this point in the story? How would you have reacted if you were on hand as Jesus died for the sins of the world? The suffering of our Lord is sad, indeed, but it is the good news of our salvation!

The story is important! Pay attention!

The Mockery

Then the soldiers of the governor took Jesus into the governor's
headquarters, and they gathered the whole cohort around him.
They stripped him and put a scarlet robe on him,
and after twisting some thorns into a
crown, they put it on his head.
They put a reed in his right hand and knelt before him
and mocked him, saying, "Hail, King of the Jews!"
They spat on him, and took the reed and struck him on the head.
After mocking him, they stripped him of the robe
and put his own clothes on him.
Then they led him away to crucify him.
(Matthew 27:27–31)

The scene is the Pavement. It was a broad stone, mosaic floor, between
the fortress of Antonia, Pilate's headquarters, and the Temple. It
was large enough to host several hundred people. Pilate lived at
Antonia when he was in Jerusalem, and there were barracks for
Roman soldiers as well. The Pavement was also a location where the
Roman troops might gather to get their orders, to drill, or to stand
for inspection. This was where the Roman governor would usually
pronounce judgment upon criminals, though rarely this early in the
morning.

Jesus had been tried through the dark hours of the night by the
chief priests and the elders before a hastily called assembly of the
Sanhedrin, the Jewish council of elders in Jerusalem. And it was
there that Jesus was convicted of blasphemy. They brought Jesus to

this place, the Pavement, to be judged by Pilate. Pilate did not put Jesus on trial; his purpose was only to hand down judgment. And even though Pilate could see through their politically mixed motives, and that Jesus was not really condemnable, he let them have their way, released Barabbas, and handed Jesus over to the soldiers whose task it would be to carry out the gruesome punishment of crucifixion.

But before handing Him over, Pilate had Jesus flogged. It was kind of a last-ditch effort to wield some control in the situation and perhaps to assuage the Jewish leaders. It seems horrible to imagine that a whipping post would have been located in such a public place, but it was a Roman place as much as a Jewish place, and any soldier who failed to do his duty might likewise be flogged before a gathering of the troops to be an example of what might happen when you either disobeyed or failed to fulfill your orders.

Jesus was tied or chained to the whipping post and given thirty-nine lashes that would have flailed the skin off His back, left Him bleeding and in incredible pain, and, for most humans, barely alive. But Jesus was surrendered. Silent. Perhaps even stoic. I believe He probably never even cried out in agony. Though I can't help but imagine He would wince with every lashing of the whip. Some scholars suggest that there could have been two soldiers flogging Jesus. With two men wielding whips, He wouldn't have any time to catch His breath between blows. The shock of one slap of the cat-o'-nine-tails would be followed immediately by another and another until thirty-nine blows were delivered. Thirty-nine was the stopping point because forty lashes were too many. The victim might die.

After Jesus was flogged, they dragged Him away. The scene changes from the place called the Pavement to the Praetorium— inside the governor's headquarters. There, the whole cohort of soldiers was gathered around Jesus (v. 27). That's when they got really mean. They taunted Jesus. A few soldiers gathered some thorny twigs, twisted them into a crown, and forced it into position on Jesus's head. More blood. More pain. Did the soldier who plaited the thorns together get pricked by them? Did he bleed too? It would seem only natural—he couldn't avoid it.

The whole idea of mocking someone is to reduce them to nothing, to shame them, to dishonor them to the point of complete humiliation. I can imagine them saying, "You say you are the king of the Jews? Here's your royal robe! Here's a scepter for you! And here's a crown! Wear it, king! We kneel before you, king! Hail, king of the Jews!" And they spat on him, took the reed they put in His hand for a scepter and whacked Him on the head with it, forcing the thorns deeper into His scalp. They mocked Him to their own shame.

Jesus was surrendered. Silent. I wonder if He looked at His abusers and if that look sparked any remorse. Sometimes a look of pity from the abused person cuts just as deep. But these men were hardened. They were the crucifiers. Jesus was nothing to them—yet!

What they did fulfilled prophetic scripture. Isaiah 53:3–10a says,

> He was despised and rejected by others; a man of suffering and acquainted with infirmity; and as one from whom others hide their faces ... he was despised, and we held Him of no account. Surely He has born our infirmities and carried our diseases; yet we accounted Him stricken, struck down by God, and afflicted. But He was wounded for our transgressions, crushed for our iniquities; upon Him was the punishment that made us whole, and by His bruises we are healed. All we like sheep have gone astray; we have all turned to our own way, and the Lord has laid on Him the iniquity of us all. He was oppressed, and He was afflicted, yet he did not open His mouth; like a lamb that is led to the slaughter, and like a sheep that before its shearers is silent, so he did not open His mouth.
>
> By a perversion of justice he was taken away. Who could have imagined His future? For He was cut off from the land of the living, stricken for the transgression of my people. They made His grave with the wicked and His tomb with the rich; although

He had done no violence, and there was no deceit in
His mouth, yet it was the will of the Lord to crush
Him with pain …

When we think of the agony our Lord endured on our behalf, it should make us extremely grateful. His torture was so severe because my sin is so terrible. Jesus suffered to take away my sin from before the throne of judgment. Jesus endured the mockery I deserve.

Ever since he began to pray in the garden of Gethsemane and His sweat became like great drops of blood (Luke 22:44), He was made into the vessel that was poured the stain of my sin and the pain of my guilt; and. … the stain of your sin and the pain of your guilt. We are forgiven by His suffering. We are redeemed by His blood!

Thank you, Jesus!

The Cross

"As they came out,
they came upon a man from Cyrene named Simon; t
hey compelled this man to carry his cross."
(Matthew 27:32)

Usually a man condemned to be crucified was forced to carry his own cross to the site where he would experience the torture of being nailed to it with large spikes and then elevated into position for all to see and to watch him suffer and die. He carried his own cross to identify him as a criminal, one deserving of this punishment—the guilty one. But Jesus had been awake for at least twenty-four hours. He had been dragged from the Mount of Olives into Jerusalem, made to stand before the Sanhedrin for hours, and then dragged before Pilate. Then, Roman soldiers had flogged Jesus to within a few inches of His life.

Jesus was probably exhausted. He could have fainted at any moment. It seems only natural to imagine that the walk to Golgotha was just too much for Him, and we can easily picture Him collapsing under the weight of His cross. Did He actually fall? Is that why Simon was conscripted to carry the cross? None of the gospels say that Jesus fell on the way out of the city. Not even once. But we can't help but try to fill in the gaps of the story and suggest His falling under the weight of the wood as the reason that Simon was tagged to fulfill this task.

Francis of Assisi and the Franciscan Order developed the legend of Jesus having fallen three times before Simon was forced to carry the cross. They developed the devotional exercise of praying the "stations" of the cross during the season of Lent and Passion week and especially on Good Friday. Regardless of whether or not Jesus fell before Simon began to carry the cross, Simon *did* begin to carry the cross! It must have had an extremely profound effect on him. I say this because scholars presume that, because Mark's telling of the story at this point mentions the small fact that Simon was the father of Alexander and Rufus (Mark 15:21), they must have been fairly well-known among the brothers and sisters of the early Christian community and were Christians themselves; therefore, Simon must have become a follower.

You are creatively compelled to imagine their father, back in Cyrene, a city in North Africa in what is now Libya, telling them about Jesus, and that he, their father, had helped Him carry His cross. No dialogue between Jesus and Simon is given in the gospels, but often, the cinematic portrayals of this scene show Simon receiving a sort of penetrating look from Jesus that compels such sympathy and mercy that Simon wants to do whatever he can to help the condemned man. It's as if, without speaking a word, Jesus assures Simon that it will be okay, that this is God's plan, that Jesus needs this small, final token of gracious and loving assistance, and so, sometimes, Simon is depicted as taking up the cross as a privilege and an honor.

Simon was a pilgrim. Scholars depict him as coming to Jerusalem to experience the Passover. He is entering the Holy City in a spirit of devotion and a spirit of faith. The sun had just risen on the new day, and the first thing he wanted to do was go to the Temple to pray. But this procession of criminals moving down the street (and it was probably downhill most of the way) interrupted his peace and upset his state of mind. He was offended by this unclean and unfaithful activity, even though he probably would have recognized the elders of the Sanhedrin by their clothing, walking close behind. And rather than stand as a spectator and watch, he may even have tried to blend into the background and face the wall to avoid seeing.

But he was noticed. For whatever reason, the soldiers chose him to bear the cross the rest of the way. Initially, he probably felt a strong sense of revulsion. No one would want to carry the cross of a criminal. No one would want to be identified with this man's guilt, or condemnation. It might even seem as if *he* was the one who would be crucified!

He didn't know the man, but you can't say no to a Roman soldier. He reluctantly entered the cause he deplored. The cross was now in his hands. Was there blood on it? Had blood soaked through the robe of Christ and smeared the wood a bit? Had blood trickled down from Jesus's head where the thorns had pierced His scalp? Suddenly, Simon had blood on his hands, and he began to wonder. Who is this man? Why has He been flogged? Why was He wearing a crown of thorns? Why was He being crucified? All these questions probably flashed through his mind in an instant. And then he looked at the man for whom he would carry a cross.

Had he heard about Jesus? Would he have known or guessed it was Him? Had the people he'd met on his pilgrimage to Jerusalem spoken about a Savior? Maybe he had overheard people talking. Maybe even, just then, Jesus—brutalized and exhausted—looked at him. Perhaps the expression in His eyes showed pity on Simon. Perhaps, without a word, Jesus gave him a look that not only said, "I'm sorry you have to do this," but "Bless you for helping me!"

He carried the cross out of the city. At Golgotha, the Romans had him drop it near where it would be raised. Then they probably pushed him out of their way. What did he do then? I imagine him stunned to have been drawn into the action. All he probably could do was stand there at first. His pilgrimage would have been spoiled. His clothes would have had bloodstains. There would have been blood on his hands. He became absorbed into the crowd and looked on. The Romans were taking out the nails. One had a hammer in his hand. He couldn't bear to watch, but he couldn't look away.

The cross is remembered more seriously during Lent. Everywhere there are Christians, there are crosses. They remind us of our Savior, of His suffering, of His death. For most people, the crosses they see are little more than symbols of their faith. But think seriously—what does the cross mean to you? What does it do for you? Is it on a necklace that you wear to identify yourself as a believer?

Roman Catholics have crucifixes—that's a cross with Christ still on it. Protestants don't leave Him there. Our crosses are empty because Jesus was not left there. Our focus is more on the Resurrection than on the suffering of Jesus. No, the story doesn't end with the suffering. We must never forget it.

Jesus suffered for our sins. He was raised for our redemption, but His Crucifixion, His death opens the gates of the prison of sin, and we are freed. The cross makes a difference!

"The Word of the cross is folly to those who are perishing, but to us who are being saved it is the power of God" (1 Corinthians 1:18).

The Suffering of the Cross

As they went out, they came upon a man
from Cyrene named Simon;
they compelled him to carry his cross.
And when they came to a place called Golgotha
(which means Place of a Skull),
they offered him wine to drink, mixed with gall;
but when he tasted it, he would not drink it.
And when they had crucified him,
they divided his clothes among themselves by casting lots;
then they sat down there and kept watch over him.
Over his head they put the charge against him, which read,
"This is Jesus, the King of the Jews."
Then two bandits were crucified with him,
one on his right and one on his left.
Those who passed by derided him, shaking their heads
and saying, "You who would destroy the
temple and rebuild it in three days,
save yourself! If you are the Son of God,
come down from the cross."
In the same way the chief priests also,
along with the scribes and elders,
were mocking him, saying,
"He saved others; he cannot save himself.
He is the King of Israel;
let him come down from the cross now, and we will believe in him.

He trusts in God; let God deliver him now, if he wants to;
for he said, 'I am God's Son.'"
The bandits who were crucified with him
also taunted him in the same way.
From noon on,
darkness came over the whole land
until three in the afternoon.
And about three o'clock Jesus cried out with a loud voice,
"Eli, Eli, lema sabachthani?" that is,
"My God, my God, why have you forsaken me?"
When some of the bystanders heard it, they said,
"This man is calling Elijah."
At once one of them ran and got a sponge, filled it with sour wine,
put it on a stick, and gave it to him to drink.
But others said,
"Wait, let us see whether Elijah will come to save him."
Then Jesus cried again with a loud voice
and breathed his last.
(Matthew 27:32–50)

Simon of Cyrene, a man coming into Jerusalem as Jesus was being brought out to be crucified, was given the cross of Christ and compelled to carry it to a place called Golgotha. What does it mean to you that he shared in the suffering of Christ or that some of the blood of Jesus that rubbed onto the cross got on Simon? And what would it mean to share in his suffering?

Paul proclaimed, in his letter to the church in Philippi, that: "For his sake I have suffered the loss of all things and count them as refuse, in order that I may gain Christ and may share in his suffering, becoming like him In his death, that, if possible, I may attain the Resurrection …" (Philippians 3:8, 10b–11).

Can we become like Jesus in death, having a faith so committed that we could say, "Father, into thy hands I commend my spirit" (Luke 23:46)? Timothy said, "The saying is sure: If we have died with him, we will also live with him; if we endure, we will also reign with him; if we deny him, he will also deny us; if we are faithless, he remains faithful—for he cannot deny himself" (2Timothy 2:11–13).

He cannot deny himself. That he died for sinners can never be denied! It is we who deny. It is we who deride him, mocking him, saying, "He saved others. He cannot save himself" (Matthew 27:42). But his suffering is our salvation. The way Peter said it was, "By his wounds we are healed" (1 Peter 2:24). It is not that He couldn't save Himself, but that He was saving others! He was making a sacrifice. As He suffered, we were forgiven. As He died, we were made alive. Peter said, "He bore our sins on his body upon the cross" (1 Peter 2:24). "Behold the Lamb of God who takes away the sins of the world" (John 1:29). Christ suffered for my sins. Jesus gave His life that we might never die.

His was a perfect sacrifice.

And what would you sacrifice? What would you give up for the sake of others? Could you ask a friend to make a sacrifice for the sake of others? How about your own son? "My God, my God, why hast thou forsaken me?" (Matthew 27:46).

Salvation!

The Crucifixion

And when they came to a place called Golgotha
(which means "place of the skull"),
they offered him wine to drink, mixed with gall;
but when he tasted it, he would not drink it.
And when they crucified him,
they divided his clothes among themselves by casting lots;
then they sat down there and kept watch over him.
Over his head they put the charge against him, which read,
"This is Jesus, the King of the Jews."
Then two bandits were crucified with him, one on his
right and one on his left. (Matthew 27:33–38)

"The message of the cross is foolishness to those who are perishing, but to those who are being saved it is the power of God" (1 Corinthians 1:18). "Jews demand signs and Greeks look for wisdom, but we preach Christ crucified: a stumbling block to Jews and foolishness to Gentiles, but to those whom God has called, both Jews and Greeks, Christ is the power of God and the wisdom of God. For the foolishness of God is wiser than human wisdom, and the weakness of God is stronger than human weakness" (1 Corinthians 1:22–25).

Nobody likes the Crucifixion, and yet it is a center point around which the Christian faith revolves. We may want to say that the Resurrection is *the* center point, but the Resurrection is the *proof* that what happened at the cross is true. The Resurrection may make us feel good, positive, hopeful, and encouraged, but the Crucifixion is what saves us from sin. No other religion, no philosophy, no ideology in the whole world deals with sin in a more complete way than what happened to Christ on a cross on that Friday so long ago. The Resurrection and the sending of the Holy Spirit affirm that Jesus is who He said He was—the Son of God!

That was the Son of God, the incarnation of God ...who was flogged, mocked, spit on, made to wear a crown of thorns, forced to go to Golgotha, and nailed to the cross, bleeding, suffering, and dying to save the world from sin. That's why the word of the cross seems like foolishness. A God who died? The eternal Creator of the universe, the ultimate source of all reality died on a cross? No logic, no rational dialectic, no moral deliberation can explain why God would suffer and die for me. But neither can you explain why someone would run into a burning building to save a stranger. Only grace can explain it all. Grace is goodness in the midst of evil, light in the midst of darkness, love in the midst of hate, and courage in the midst of danger. Grace brings us **God's Riches At Christ's Expense!** G.R.A.C.E.

Simon of Cyrene helped Jesus get the cross to Golgotha. *Calvary* is from the Latin. Both mean the same thing: "the place of the skull." Some say there was a rock formation there that resembled a skull. But it was a place where crucifixions occurred often and was known as a place of death. To call it "the place of the skull" seems a fitting nickname anyway. And it was there that Jesus was crucified.

First, before anything was done to Christ, they offered Him "wine mixed with gall" (Matthew 27:34). This was a sort of pain-relieving palliative that would often make the suffering last longer. Some say Jesus refused it to feel every pang of agony as He suffered. The assumption is that the more aware God might be of the human suffering endured by Jesus, the more perfect God's redeeming grace might be. The cost of our ransom was truly paid in full! I don't feel the necessity of all that, but it *can* make sense. I just think the process didn't need prolonging any more than it already was. Our ransom, our redemption was paid by Jesus Christ—by His death and by His suffering. Not by how much pain He suffered or how dead He became. The palliative is mentioned in the gospels simply because it was done. It was not mentioned in Luke. In John, Jesus accepts it!

The act of crucifying Jesus is barely mentioned. It obviously took a central place in the scene, but all it says is, "When they had crucified Him ..." (v. 35). Our minds picture the process passing in a sort of hushed silence except for the nails, the hammer, and the cruel indifference of the Roman soldiers. Perhaps there were even occasional comments made by some who were watching. There might have been crying women among the spectators. There were probably cries of agony from both Christ and the robbers as the nails pierce their flesh. Sometimes, we feel like spectators witnessing something horrible. But we can't take the Crucifixion casually. It is the most powerful reality in history, along with the Resurrection. The word of the cross is the power of God! We preach Christ crucified! (1 Corinthians 1:23).

"They divided His clothes by casting lots" (v. 35a). Whatever is meant by "casting lots," dice, names, or tokens in a hat, the last few things that belonged to Jesus became the belongings of others. Done directly within view of the victim, it's another stab of mockery meant to reduce the victim to nothing. It was done. It was part of a crucifixion. And it fulfills a passage of scripture from Psalm 22:18. The psalm is like a nightmare being remembered, interlaced with hope and praise, encouragement and faith. But it is considered to be a vision of a crucifixion. And it expresses fairly vividly the agony experienced.

Matthew 27:37 then shares about the "titulus" that was posted near the top of the cross over the head of Jesus. A *titulus* is a sign. At a crucifixion, a sign with the words of the victim's crime written on it was added for passersby to witness the reason this person was being punished. Often, today, we see *INRI*. Latin didn't have *J*s, so *Jesus* becomes *Iesus*, and *Jews* is *Iudaerum*. *INRI* stands for "Jesus of Nazareth, King of the Jews." The *R* is for *Rex*. *Iesus Nazarenus Rex Iudaerum*. It's like an epitaph. And though an epitaph on a headstone is usually fairly positive, this was all Jesus got. His crime before the powers of Rome was His claim to be a king. That was an act of treason. As far as the Jews were concerned, Jesus's crime was blasphemy because He claimed to be the Son of God. Roman authorities like Pilate wouldn't have cared about local theological issues, so the elders accused Jesus of claiming to be a king. Still, Pilate not only saw through them; he didn't think that Jesus was really guilty of anything other than annoying the Jewish elders. But Jesus *had* admitted that He was the king of the Jews (27:11).

The final act of this scene is the crucifixion of two robbers on either side of Jesus. Why their punishment was added to the punishment of Jesus is not known. Perhaps it was just a matter of expedience: "Let's deal with these two while we're at it." One crucifixion was horrible. Three would have magnified the agony and shown the gathering crowds coming into Jerusalem an example of how they'd better not mess with the Roman powers. It was known that they would crucify practically any person for just looking at them the wrong way.

Power can be very oppressive. But the power of the cross can be very liberating. At the cross, the burden of our sin is taken away. At the cross, the power of sin is defeated. At the cross, the suffering we deserve is paid for. Jesus Christ is our Savior, our redeemer, our ransom, our substitution, and our atoning sacrifice! Jesus is "the Lamb of God who takes away the sin of the world" (John 1:29). He paid the price. He paid it all, and we receive God's riches at Christ's expense!

Galatians 2:19b–20 says, "I have been crucified with Christ; it is no longer I who live, but Christ who lives in me. And the life I now live in the flesh I live by faith in the Son of God, who loved me and gave Himself for me."

The Taunting

Those who passed by derided him, shaking their heads and saying,
"You who would destroy the temple and build it in three days,
save yourself!
If you are the Son of God, come down from the cross."
In the same way the chief priests also,
along with the scribes and elders,
were mocking him, saying, "He saved others;
he cannot save himself.
He is the king of Israel;
let him come down from the cross now,
and we will believe in him.
He trusts in God; let God deliver him now, if he wants to;
for he said, 'I am God's Son.'"
The bandits who were crucified with him also taunted
him in the same way. (Matthew 27:39–44)

Have you ever been mocked or taunted for something you've said or done? Sometimes it's a matter of the values you hold or the morals you claim. Sometimes, it might have something to do with your looks, your size, or your clothes, or even because of where you're from. It can be downright abusive. I had red hair (auburn). (At this stage of my life, I still claim that I do). And I was teased a few hundred times because of it. I didn't really care because I was far more often complimented than taunted. But in college, I knew girls who were mocked for not wanting to lose their virginity. I was mocked for being religious. Others were mocked for never getting drunk. People could be very unkind and ungracious.

My heart was bruised one time when I suggested, after a friend had very casually used God's name in vain as he described something he thought was a stupid thing to do, that instead of saying what he did, he could have just used the word *crummy* or *rotten*. In response, that person took God's name in vain over and over again in place of every needed adjective. I just got up, looked at my friend with righteous disdain, and walked away. That person was no longer my friend, and likewise for the guys who laughed at me with him. I just chalked it up to their ignorance, and it was their loss because they had all lost my friendship.

Jesus was taunted when He was on the cross. It was the worst few hours of His life. He was dying, and their mockery had malicious intent. They might have thought it was funny, if not just cruel, as they flung their verbal insults at Jesus. But their taunts said more about them than it did about Jesus.

I suppose a reason for mocking someone might be to "put him or her in his or her place," at least in the mocker's mind. But there is a twisted sort of joy in trying to do so. Not letting it get to us can also be a way to turn their taunts back at them. When I've watched cinematic depictions of this scene from the Crucifixion, I've wanted to have laser beams shoot out of Jesus's eyes to disintegrate His mockers. But Jesus had said, "Father, forgive them" (Luke 34:34). Not in the gospel of Matthew, though. Matthew draws a picture of such total abandonment and condemnation that it hurts to read this part of the story. Perhaps he writes it this way to show the very deep contrast between Jesus and those who rejected Him. God gets the last laugh, though, when the mockers are left totally dumfounded on Sunday after Jesus rises from the dead.

The Revised Standard Version uses the word *derided* when Matthew tells us that, "Those passing by *derided* him" (v. 39). The word could also have been translated as *blasphemed*. We, who are believers hearing this story, can feel that truth because we know that Jesus is God, and they are speaking against our Lord. They mock

Jesus for having said He could rebuild the temple in three days if it was destroyed. "You said it, so, save yourself" (v. 40). It's as if they are thinking, "If you have the power you say you do, use it!" They said, "If you are the Son of God, come down from the cross" (v. 40b).

The chief priests pile on, along with the scribes and elders, the hypocritical leaders of the faith, "mocking him, saying, 'He saved others; he cannot save himself. He is the king of Israel; let him come down from the cross now, and we will believe in him,'" (vv. 41–42). We need to hear the harsh sarcasm in their tones of voice. But often, behind sarcasm, there is truth. I wonder if they were, in a bitter way, acknowledging the grace of God in Jesus when they said, "He saved others ..." Had they seen this attitude in the testimony of Christ's followers? Did they purposefully reject the saving grace they had seen In Jesus's forgiving words and ways?

"He cannot save himself" (v. 42). Do their words imply the notion that Jesus was "unable" to save Himself? I've known a few people who have thought that all they can do is save themselves. They feel no sense of a larger purpose for their beliefs. With such an attitude, every effort of mission work, every hope of leading others to Christ, and every desire to "make disciples of all nations" (Matthew 28:19), would be thought of as a waste of time and energy. It's as if they think the only purpose of faith is getting a ticket to heaven! Wrong! Surely, however, Jesus was able, but, He chose to suffer. And we, likewise, need to deny ourselves and take up our crosses.

Think of doctors. They do not train and develop skills in order to save themselves. Some might be mocked with the proverbial phrase, "Doctor, cure yourself" (Luke 4:23). Jesus acknowledged that notion when some of the people of His hometown didn't want to accept Him as anything special. But the idea is that doctors aren't in the healing business for their own sakes, but rather, for the sakes of others. Jesus would not "save himself." It was not His purpose. The reason Jesus did not save Himself from suffering and death was precisely to save others. This truth should not be mocked. I thank God that Jesus Christ took my sins upon Himself and suffered in my place.

"He trusts in God; let God deliver him now, if he wants to; for he said, 'I am God's Son'" (v. 43). They thought they were taunting Jesus, but that's exactly what happened. It just didn't happen on that Friday. Trust God even when you are suffering. Of course, that's not what the "bandits" did, who were crucified with Jesus. They taunted Him too. Sometimes, when we are suffering, we lash out. Jesus was the easy target. It is only in Luke that one of those criminals repents and asks Jesus to "remember" him (Luke 23:42). They could just as easily have lashed out at the Roman soldiers (and maybe they did), but, hey, *they* still had the hammer! We need to deny ourselves, and take up our crosses.

The travesty of this scene is the blatant wickedness of the religious leaders who put in their digs. Matthew certainly made them look bad. They're cruel and mean-spirited. It takes no faith at all to taunt someone who is suffering. They should have recognized the Messiah when they saw Him. Instead, they saw Jesus as a political and moral threat to their power and prestige and integrity.

The greatest lesson is that mockery accomplishes absolutely nothing good.

The Cry of Forsakenness

> From noon on, darkness came over the whole
> land until three in the afternoon. And about
> three o'clock Jesus cried with a loud voice,
> "Eli, Eli, lema sabachthani?" that is,
> "My God, my God, why have you forsaken me?"
> When some of the bystanders heard it, they said,
> "This man is calling for Elijah."
> At once one of them ran and got a sponge,
> filled it with sour wine, put it on a stick,
> and gave it to him to drink.
> But others said,
> "Wait, let us see whether Elijah will come to save him."
> (Matthew 27:45–49)

The ninth plague in the story of Exodus is a plague of darkness, "a darkness that could be felt" (Exodus 10:21). There is a time when darkness is not just an absence of light, but the presence of gloom—a numb sort of shadow or a dim blackness. It penetrates the heart and obscures the mind. The darkness that surrounded Jerusalem from noon till three o'clock was like that.

It got quiet; God was dying. Jesus Christ, the Son of God, the incarnation of God, was failing. His breaths were shallow and slow; His heart rate was negligible; and His eyes were dilating. He could no longer feel, but He was lingering. In those hours, God was suffering all the pain of all the guilt that sin had caused and would cause in the future. It was poured into Him like a rising tide or a flood. It washed through Him like a waterfall; it filled Him like an overdose, forcing itself upon Him and gorging Him till He couldn't help but burst. In Matthew 27:46, He cried out, "Eli, Eli, lema sabachthani?" (My God, my God, why have You forsaken me?)

The piercing darkness was shattered by a cry of abandonment, forsakenness. All my sin, all my guilt was added to all your sin and all your guilt and to all the sin and guilt of every soul ever to inhabit the Earth. How could Jesus not feel forsaken? In the body of Jesus, God summoned up a final surge of agony for the world to hear and for Golgotha to receive. Jesus was so completely surrendered to this purpose that God abandoned Him. God abandoned Himself for me and for you. It was all God could do in that human body at its end. God cried out. God Himself felt forsaken so that we could know that we are not.

The sudden, startled shock of His outcry jolted the nearby people to attention. They heard what Jesus said, but they didn't hear it clearly. It sounded, to some, like Jesus was crying out for Elijah. Elijah had never died. He was taken up into heaven by a whirlwind in a chariot of fire (2 Kings 2:11–12), but Elijah would return. The Old Testament ends by God telling us, "Behold, I will send you the prophet Elijah before the great and dreadful day of the Lord comes" (Malachi 4:5).

Was this it? Could Jesus be summoning Elijah? Let's rouse Him! Get the vinegar! Get a sponge! Hold it up to His nose so He can breathe its odor; hold it to His mouth so He can taste its sharp kick. This was a caustic stimulant, meant to rouse someone the way smelling salts invigorate a person. Perhaps they thought that somehow, Elijah, the greatest of the prophets, who had miraculously resuscitated the son of a poor widow (2 Kings 17:17–24), would arrive and that he would open the skies and swoop down in the chariot of fire to do something incredible or spectacular!

But Jesus had never called for Elijah. He felt so alone that He cried out, completely forlorn, completely deserted, desolate. Life was ebbing away from the life-giver. The holy one took on unholiness! Jesus was dying of more than blood loss, more than asphyxiation. His

Spirit was being morally crushed. Because He took sin upon Himself, Jesus became the Lamb that was slain for the sin of the world—for my sins, for your sins. Thanks be to God!

What does it mean to you that Jesus felt forsaken? What does it mean to you that He was suffering and dying for your sins? How does His suffering make you feel? What will you do now because of it?

The Death and the Earthquake

Then Jesus cried again with a loud voice and breathed his last.
At that moment
the curtain of the temple was torn in two, from top to bottom.
The earth shook, and the rocks were split.
The tombs also were opened,
and many bodies of the saints who had fallen asleep were raised.
After his Resurrection
they came out of the tombs and entered the
holy city and appeared to many.
Now when the centurion and those with him,
who were keeping watch over Jesus,
saw the earthquake and what took place,
they were terrified and said,
"Truly this man was God's Son!"
(Matthew 27:50–54)

Earthquakes happen when there is a shift in tectonic plates deep beneath the surface of the Earth. At the moment of Christ's death, deep beneath the surface of all existence, there was a shift so significant that there was a seismic experience that could be felt. Like the darkness that surrounded Jerusalem and perhaps the whole land—a darkness that could be felt; likewise, this seismic shift was precisely that substantial. It could be felt. In the spiritual and moral realm, a shift in the effect of sin happened. Sin was buried so deep, and righteousness was elevated so high that all of life became different. The innocence of Christ was that pure, and His sacrifice for sin was that perfect! The curtain of the Temple, the barrier between the holy place with the altar and the Holy of Holies—the holiest place where the Ark of the Covenant, which contained the tablets of the Ten Commandments—was eliminated. The notion that anything stood between God and His likeness in humanity was altered. Sin may have made that barrier necessary for the protection of humankind from the fire of God's total holiness, but now, sin was dealt with in such a final way that, in a manner of speaking, the human spirit became inflammable. The effect of sin was so completely diminished for the faithful that they were set free from it!

The power of sin is not gone; guilt and the prospect of a negative afterlife may still exist for the unfaithful. But in that single moment, Christ dealt with sin in such a perfect way that even death was overcome briefly for the saints who had died. Tombs broke open, and those who had lived holy lives were raised later, after the Resurrection, and appeared to many people in Jerusalem!

God, in Christ, summoned up one last outcry, and Jesus gave up the Spirit. His body was dead. The heart of God-incarnate stopped beating and He breathed His last breath. It was over. It was finished. But *it* was just beginning! Simultaneous with that cry of Christ, the earthquake came, the curtain ripped, the rocks split, the tombs opened, and the saints awakened!

Already, existence was different. There would be another earthquake at the moment of the Resurrection, when another seismic shift in the spiritual realm occurred, but this divine act, the completion of Christ's Sacrifice—His death—has changed things so considerably in the moral reality of life, that our acceptance of that sacrifice for our souls washes us clean. Oh, we can still get dirty, but the grace and power of God's reconciliation and our repentance returns us to a state of cleanliness. We are set free from sin. Hallelujah!

We experience this seismic shift in our lives when we acknowledge our brokenness—the sacrifice acceptable to God is a broken spirit! "A broken and contrite heart, O God, You will not despise" (Psalm 51:17). Then we can seek God's grace and discover God's forgiveness.

Faith helps us identify in such a way with what Christ has done that we can say with Paul, "I have been crucified with Christ. It is no longer I who live, but Christ who lives in me" (Galatians 2:20). But we need to look at Christ on the cross and see our sins and our guilt being taken to the grave. "Those who belong to Christ Jesus have crucified their sinful nature" (Galatians 5:24).

Becoming faithful is like changing our clothes. "As many of you as were baptized into Christ have clothed yourselves with Christ" (Galatians 3:27). "You were taught to put away your former way of life, your old self, corrupt and deluded by its lusts, and to be renewed in the spirit of your minds, and to clothe yourselves with the new self, created according to the likeness of God in true righteousness and holiness" (Ephesians 4:22–24). "If we have been united with Jesus in a death like His, we will certainly be united with Him in a Resurrection like His. We know that our old self was crucified with Him so that the body of sin might be destroyed, and we might no longer be enslaved to sin" (Romans 6:5–6). "The death He died, He died to sin, once for all; but the Life He lives He lives to God. So you also must consider yourselves dead to sin and alive to God in Christ Jesus" (Romans 6:10–11).

Our nature is different! 2 Corinthians 5:17 says, "If anyone is in Christ, they are a new creation; the old has died! Behold, the new has come!" We will now walk in the light as Christ is in the light (1 John 1:7). We can claim what Christ has claimed: "In the world, you will have tribulation; but take heart! I have overcome the world" (John 16:33).

And the centurion at the foot of the cross, he heard Christ's final cry, felt the earthquake, saw the rocks split, and knew and announced it: "Truly this Man was God's Son" (27:54). He was the first Gentile believer.

Faith is not just about hope and heaven. Heaven begins now. Faith is about change—changed hearts, changed minds, and saved souls. It happened at the cross! Galatians 6:14 says, "May I never boast except in the cross of our Lord Jesus Christ, through whom the world has been crucified to me, and I to the world!"

Dead and Buried

Many women were also there, looking on from a distance;
they followed Jesus from Galilee and had provided for him.
Among them were Mary Magdalene,
and Mary the mother of James and Joseph,
and the mother of the sons of Zebedee.
When it was evening,
there came a rich man from Arimathea, named Joseph,
who was a disciple of Jesus.
He went to Pilate and asked for the body of Jesus;
then Pilate ordered it to be given to him.
So Joseph took the body and wrapped it in a clean linen cloth
and laid it in his own new tomb, which had been hewn in the rock.
He then rolled a great stone to the door of the tomb and went away.
Mary Magdalene and the other Mary were
there, sitting opposite the tomb.
The next day, that is, after the day of preparation,
the chief priests and the Pharisees gathered before Pilate and said,
"Sir, we remember what that imposter said while he was still alive,
'After three days I will rise again.'
Therefore command the tomb to be made
secure until the third day;
otherwise his disciples may go and steal him away,
and tell people, 'He has been raised from the dead,'
and the last deception would be worse than the first."
Pilate said to them, "You have a guard of soldiers;

go, make it as secure as you can."
So they went with the guard and made the tomb
secure by sealing the stone. (Matthew 27:55–66)

The end of the story? Not! We know it's not over. *We* know the rest of the story. We're even part of it now. We are believers, Christians. Jesus was dead and buried. *They* thought it was over. They did everything they could to put a period at the end of the sentence. He was buried. "They went with the guard and made the tomb secure by sealing the stone" (Matthew 27:66).

But we know—not just because there's still another chapter in the gospel of Matthew, but because Jesus rose! There *is* more to the story. If He didn't rise, we all would have been fooled. Paul said, "If for this life only we have hoped in Christ, we are of all people most to be pitied" (1 Corinthians 15:19).

The world wants to leave Jesus in the tomb. We, who believe, have heard the angel say it over and over: "He is not here. He has been raised" (Matthew 28:6). But for those few who can't believe it or won't believe it because they are too practical—so practical that they scoff at the idea of miracles, at the notion of mystery, or at the amazement of wonder—they won't let go of what they see as flaws in the story or inconsistencies between the gospels. Some might be intellectually unwilling to accept anything that suggests that the spiritual is real, or, that the soul exists, let alone, is eternal. They think they're too intelligent to fall for this stuff. It is not a matter of intelligence, it is a matter of a lack of trust, a lack of faith.

So, why did they need a guard? Because they thought, "His disciples may go and steal Him away and tell the people, 'He has been raised from the dead,' and the last deception would be worse than the first" (Matthew 27:64). How arrogant! And yet how practical. They thought they could be smarter than God!

Read 1 Corinthians 1:18–25:

> For the message about the cross is foolishness to those
> who are perishing, but to us who are being saved it

is the power of God. For it is written, 'I will destroy the wisdom of the wise, and the discernment of the discerning I will thwart.' Where is the one who is wise? Where is the debater of this age? Has not God made foolish the wisdom of the world? For since, in the wisdom of God, the world did not know God through wisdom, God decided, through the foolishness of our proclamation, to save those who believe. For Jews demand signs and Greeks seek wisdom, but we proclaim Christ crucified, a stumbling block to the Jews and foolishness to the Gentiles, but to those who are called, both Jews and Greeks, Christ the power of God and the wisdom of God. For God's foolishness is wiser than human wisdom, and God's weakness is stronger than human strength.

With sarcastic wit, Paul uses the notion of *foolishness* to refute human logic. And though Paul is talking about the message of the cross, the message of the Resurrection was probably even more foolish in the minds of those who couldn't fathom the reality of someone rising from the dead. Logic cannot interpret human experience, let alone begin to understand divine purposes. That's where the chief priests and the Pharisees were stuck. Foolishness!

"Many women were there ..." (Matthew 27:55). They had watched Jesus die. They had heard the words spoken by the centurion at the moment of His death: "Truly this man was God's Son" (Matthew 27:54). Some of them are named by Matthew. After the Sabbath (according to Matthew), two of the Marys went to the tomb. Perhaps they had already begun discussing how they might honor Jesus when the time was right.

Meanwhile, another practical man, Joseph of Arimathea, thought clearly enough to do the functional work of taking Jesus's body and laying it his own newly excavated tomb. The two Marys saw it all. Joseph was practical in that what he did was needed, while others were only wringing their hands or cowering in fear. But Joseph, though one of *them*—a member of the council of elders (Mark 15:43), was a disciple. He had seen in Jesus a truth the doubters could not see. And what he did honored Jesus.

It's not over when it's over. Love doesn't end when someone dies. Even doubters know this. Even nonbelievers. There's something wonderful within us that continues to reach out in the direction of our loved ones. It's something mysterious that can't make clear sense in this lifetime. And when we can't fully understand something, we often make up our own explanations. The chief priests and the Pharisees explained away the Resurrection by propagating the story that the disciples had stolen Jesus's body from the tomb—the last deception—and were then lying to everyone that Jesus had risen from death (27:64).

But we who believe trust the story. Our faith could not possibly be based on a lie. Jesus died for our sins, but He rose to bring us the assurance of eternal life. There comes a point when to doubt is to rebel, where being unwilling to accept the grace of God in Christ is to deny the possibilities and reject the truth. I believe that when it's over, when we have finished our course in this world and come before the gates of heaven, we will discover that our doubts were really just self-doubt. We doubted because we were not yet able to understand, and because there were things we couldn't make sense of in our limited minds, we couldn't accept the truths that others proclaimed. Paul himself confessed that, "For now we see in a mirror dimly, but then we will see face to face. Now I know only in part, then we shall understand fully ..." (1 Corinthians 13:12). With patience, we'll understand it better by and by.

For now, we know there was a time when Jesus was dead and buried, grave-guarded, stone-sealed, end of story. It was a reason to grieve. For doubters, maybe it was a reason to gloat. But that's almost two thousand years ago! Something amazing must have happened for the story to last that long.

Christ is risen! He is risen indeed!

Part III

Part III

The Passion in Luke

The story of Christ's passion in the gospel of Luke tells the same story that Matthew and Mark do. John's gospel has many details that are not in the other gospels. Of particular interest to me is the dialogue between Jesus and Pontius Pilate. And although the details in John are worth examining in depth, I will not be doing so here, for the sake of space. This book will be long enough.

But in Luke, there are several unique details that seem quite relevant when compared to Matthew and Mark. At Gethsemane, as Jesus prayed, "an angel from God appeared to Him and gave Him strength" (22:43). Jesus healed the ear of the high priest's servant after one of the disciples cut it off with a sword at the moment of Jesus's arrest (22:51). In Luke, Pilate sends Jesus to Herod to be examined (23:7–11). On the way to Golgotha, Jesus speaks to some women grieving for Him, and He says the somewhat cryptic, "If they do this when the wood is green, what will happen when it is dry?" (23:31).

In Luke, as Jesus is crucified, He says, "Father, forgive them; for they do not know what they are doing" (23:34). In Luke, one of the men crucified with Jesus repents and asks to be remembered. Jesus tells him, "Truly I tell you, today you will be with me in Paradise" (23:43).

These are important details that add to the story of the Passion. Choosing not to analyze the differences in the gospel accounts, but rather seeing them as simply coming from differing points of view, it seems important to me to let those details continue to inspire us in our meditations.

The core of the story is still solid. The extra details bring it a special depth and feeling. In Luke, though Jesus is completely abandoned, as noted in Matthew and Mark, there are these special moments that reveal something more of Christ's character, like the healing of the ear, the forgiveness for those who crucified Him, and the promise of paradise for one of the crucified men. There is compassion in the Passion.

The Passion of Christ is still hard, and it weighs heavily on our hearts as we meditate on every scene. But what is important to know is that the suffering of Jesus happened to redeem those who believe in Him. My sin is dealt with by His suffering. Thank you, Jesus.

Anguish and Arrest

You are those who have stood by me in my trials;
and I confer on you, just as my Father has conferred on me,
a kingdom,
so that you may eat and drink at my table in my kingdom,
and you will sit on thrones judging the twelve tribes of Israel.
"Simon, Simon, Listen!
Satan has demanded to sift all of you like wheat,
but I have prayed for you that your own faith may not fail;
and you, when once you have turned back,
strengthen your brothers."
And he said to him,
"Lord, I am ready to go with you to prison and to death!"
Jesus said,
"I tell you, Peter, the cock will not crow this day,
until you have denied three times that you know me."
"He said to them,
"When I sent you out without a purse, bag, or sandals,
did you lack anything?" They said, "No, not a thing."
He said to them,
"But now, the one who has a purse must take it, and likewise a bag.
And the one who has no sword must sell his cloak and buy one.
For I tell you, this scripture must be fulfilled in me,
'And he was counted among the lawless';
and indeed what is written about me is being fulfilled."
And they said, "Lord, look, here are two swords."

He replied, "It is enough."
He came out and went, as was his custom, to the Mount of Olives;
and the disciples followed him.
When he reached the place, he said to them,
"Pray that you may not come into the time of trial."
Then he withdrew from them about a stone's throw,
knelt down, and prayed,
"Father, if you are willing, remove this cup from me;
yet, not my will but yours be done."
Then an angel from heaven appeared to
him and gave him strength.
In his anguish he prayed more earnestly,
and his sweat became like great drops of
blood falling down on the ground.
When he got up from prayer,
he came to his disciples and found them sleeping because of grief,
and he said to them,
"Why are you sleeping?
Get up and pray that you may not come into the time of trial."
While he was still speaking, suddenly a crowd came,
and one called Judas, one of the twelve, was leading them.
He approached Jesus to kiss him;
but Jesus said to him,
"Judas, is it with a kiss that you are betraying the Son of Man?"
When those who were around him saw
what was coming, they asked,
"Lord, shall we strike with the sword?"
Then one of them struck the slave of the
high priest and cut off his right ear.
But Jesus said, "No more of this!"
And he touched the ear and healed him.
Then Jesus said to the chief priests, the
officers of the temple police,
and the elders who had come for him,
"Have you come out with swords and clubs as if I were a bandit?

When I was with you day after day in the temple,
you did not lay hands on me.
But this is your hour, and the power of darkness!"
(Luke 22:25–53)

"It is enough" (v. 38). Two swords were all they had. But for Jesus's purpose, it was enough. His purpose in suggesting that they prepare for battle was simply to fulfill an image of prophecy. In Isaiah 53, the suffering servant is "numbered with the transgressors" (v. 12c). Jesus cites this passage in its more common implication: "He was counted among the lawless" (22:37). In a very superficial way, it makes them look like a band of malcontents.

Their time in the upper room was over. It was dark now. They were getting ready to leave. Jesus reminded them that they lacked nothing when He sent them out to preach and heal, probably about six months to a year before His death. There is such a thing as the sufficiency of faith. When there is faith, there is enough because faith creates hope; in hope, there is joy; and with joy, there is love—a love for life such that to add anything to it is frivolous, superfluous, and unnecessary. For one who has faith, love is enough. Trust in the Lord your God. It is enough. The battle belongs to the Lord, but there will be a battle. It will be a spiritual one. And the disciples would have to pray through the worst of it. Especially Jesus.

Then this rough-and-tough, threatening group went to the Mount of Olives. There, Jesus told them to pray that they might not face the time of trial (v. 40) and to pray for the love that is enough. They had no clue, though. The deepest darkness was just setting in. They felt it; it grieved them, but it was flooding into Jesus—powerfully. He got away from them, so they didn't have to bear it, and He went about a stone's throw away. The darkness of sin, both present and future—yours and mine and for millions yet to come—was pouring into our Lord. He suffered just to feel it. Jesus was becoming sin. He prayed, but it was only the beginning. It was a horrible time of incredible anguish. Did Jesus doubt, or was He truly agonizing only over the suffering that lay ahead, as God would grieve over the evil attitudes of the sinful people in the world He'd made? (Genesis 6:6) Did God-incarnate want God the author of existence to alter the plan, or was God accepting the cup He had filled for Himself? "Not my will, but Yours be done" (v. 42). He has given us an example of self-sacrifice. And sacrificing our own best interests for the sakes of others takes nothing but a divinely inspired resolve and a divinely given strength. The suffering of Jesus had begun even before He was arrested. No wonder He was so silent during His trial.

Meanwhile, Judas was struggling with a darkness of his own, a darkness he had chosen, perhaps. How often do we choose betrayal? Not intentionally, perhaps, but by our attitudes and actions, we betray the faith we claim. Betrayal is a darkness that completely cuts off the light of grace. It sees its subject as an enemy or as a problem. Betrayal is a darkness that wants to quench the light of another. Judas let himself become engulfed by it. He led those threatened by Jesus to the Mount of Olives. He must have slipped away while the others were praying and falling asleep. And the chief priests and elders and their minions were so blinded by their own spiritual darkness that they weren't even aware of the great sin-filled darkness of that hour.

One of the disciples could see what was coming and started to wield his sword. In the eerie light of torches borne by the men in charge of Jesus's arrest, all he could accomplish was the cutting off of an ear (Luke 22:50). But again, Jesus said, "Enough!" And despite the spiritual darkness that was stirring within Him, Jesus offered one last glimmer of light: He healed that wound of the high priest's slave. "No more of this" (v. 51). There would be enough darkness that night for a thousand lifetimes.

A final word of light exposes the sin of hypocrisy in the hearts of His accusers. "Have you come out with swords and clubs as if I were a bandit? When I was with you day after day in the temple, you did not lay hands on me" (v. 52–53a). Jesus had made Himself available to them. The truth is always available; we just choose not to lay our hands on it. We can't always grasp it because we're too busy holding on to our own false ideas. We would rather not see the light. We might not like the way it makes us look at ourselves because we might not like what it reveals about us, and so we choose the darkness of our fallen states. It's what we're used to. We don't want to change. We feel as though we have *enough* light, *enough* truth, but we're blinded, and we end up living a lie. The only *enough* that truly matters is the sufficiency that comes by faith. And it is only by faith that we are able to do God's will and drink God's cup.

That night, there was so much anguish that we now see any suffering that we might have to endure as meager in comparison. And the willingness and resolve to accept the cup of sacrifice in our own lives is given strength because Jesus was given strength. We, too, can pray more earnestly. The trials may still come. Jesus was still arrested, but the promise of light is always before us, even when the darkness is deepest.

Jesus surrendered Himself. "This is your hour, and the power of darkness" (v. 53). The hour of our repentance contains the promise of light. As dark as our sins may feel, the hope for light is far more powerful!

Simon, Simon, Listen

"Simon, Simon, listen!
Satan has demanded to sift you all like wheat,
but I have prayed for you that your own faith may not fail;
and you, when once you have turned back,
strengthen your brothers."
And he said to him, "Lord, I am ready to go with
you to prison and to death!" Jesus said,
"I tell you, Peter, the cock will not crow this day,
until you have denied three times that you know me."
(Luke 22:31–34)

If your life was put into a sifter, what would be sifted through? Wheat doesn't get sifted today; it gets crushed in the mill, ground into flour, and then strained through a sifter. How is Satan crushing you, grinding you, and sifting your life? One of the things that can happen to flour after it has been sifted is that it can easily be blown away. How might it feel to consider that Satan might be thinking about how to blow you away?

In Biblical times, sifting was a part of the process of turning wheat into flour. They used baskets for this. The good wheat seeds stayed in the baskets, while the smallest pieces of chaff and the broken pieces of wheat were shaken through. Then the unusable pieces were left, and the wheat seeds were saved for grinding in a small stone mill that many families would have had. We have a glorious vision in the "Battle Hymn of the Republic" where it says: "He has sounded forth the trumpet that shall never call retreat; He is sifting out the hearts of men before His judgment seat; O be swift, my soul, to answer Him; be jubilant my feet! Our God is marching on!"

How is your heart being sifted by Christ? Before this passage, the disciples had disputed over which of them would be greatest (Luke 22:24). They were still at the table of Christ's Last Supper. And then, Jesus had something to say particularly to Peter. "Simon, Simon, listen!" Could Simon Peter have been the one who came out on top as the one who would be the greatest? Could that be the reason why Jesus focused His attention on him? "Simon, Simon, listen! Satan has demanded to sift all of you like wheat, but I have prayed for you that your own faith may not fail" (Luke 22:31–32).

How would you feel if someone told you he or she was praying for you? Would you feel offended by the implication that your faith might, in fact, fail? Imagine Job. The story of Job is about a man whom Satan sifted like wheat in an attempt to foil his loyalty to God. Job loses everything, ends up with horrible sores all over his body, and has friends come who try to convince him that he should repent since they are sure that his circumstances have come as a divine punishment for some sin he has not confessed. The climax of the tale comes when Job cries out, saying, "I know that my redeemer lives" (19:25). Job becomes impatient, though. He gets angry, wondering where God might be. And when God finally speaks with Job, He asks Job, "Will you even put me in the wrong? Will you condemn me so that you may be justified?" (Job 40:8).

I think we all do that. Rather than admit sin, the sinful natures within us, and our fallen states, we tend to ask, "Why does God let this happen to me?" We make God out to be the one who is falling short instead of grieving our sins, confessing our evils, and repenting in penitence! For what does God want us to pray? Jesus prays that our faith may not fail! Do we pray that way too?

Jesus tells Peter that Satan had demanded to sift all of the disciples like wheat, but the next *you* is singular. "I have prayed for you, Peter." Peter was the subject of Christ's prayers. "And you, Peter, when once you have turned back, strengthen your brothers" (v. 32).

From what do you need to turn back? What pulls you away from

Christ? What are the wrong directions in your life? What do you have to do to turn back? How would your life be different if you changed your ways? Don't be afraid to ask others how you should change your life to make it better. Hopefully their list won't be too long. And think about what you could do to strengthen others. How could you bolster their resolve? How would doing so strengthen you?

Listen to how Peter tried to justify himself when Jesus suggested that his faith might fail: "Lord, I am willing to go with you to prison and to death" (v. 33). Ha! We who know the rest of the story already hear only bravado, false courage—all talk. And yet, I believe it is worthy of consideration to think about how far we think we are willing to go for Christ. But that's the exact time when Jesus told Peter that "the cock will not crow this day, until you have denied three times that you know me" (v. 34). The good news is that Peter did turn back; he did strengthen the brothers. He became reconciled to the risen Jesus even after he had denied Him, and Peter became one of the greatest apostles.

How many times do we deny knowing Jesus, though? We may not say so in so many words, but our actions, our lifestyles, and our worldliness may be seen by others as evidence that we might not know Jesus as Lord in our lives. By our neglect, even without our knowing it; by our greed, our lack of self-denial by our efforts at self-preservation; or our lack of self-sacrifice—by all of this, we might be seen as people who just don't really know Jesus!

If we *do* know Him and we are ever afraid to admit it, from what fears do we need to turn back? And where can we find the strength to do so? Isn't it here? Isn't it in the fellowship of faith? Right here is the place where we can find strength with one another. Do all you can to strengthen your brothers and sisters. Satan wants to sift them like wheat. But Christ is praying for us.

Denial

Then they seized him and led him away,
bringing him into the high priest's house.
But Peter was following at a distance.
When they had kindled a fire in the middle of the
courtyard and sat down together, Peter sat among them.
Then a servant girl, seeing him in the
firelight, stared at him and said,
"This man also was with him."
But he denied it, saying, "Woman, I do not know him."
A little later someone else, on seeing him, said,
"You also are one of them,"
But Peter said, "Man, I am not!"
Then about an hour later still another man kept insisting,
"Surely this man also was with him; for he is a Galilean."
But Peter said, "Man, I do not know what you are talking about!"
At that moment, while he was speaking,
the cock crowed.
The Lord turned and looked at Peter.
Then Peter remembered the word of the
Lord, how he had said to him,
"Before the cock crows today, you will deny me three times."
And he went out and wept bitterly.
(Luke 22:54–62)

I must weep with Peter. Not because I'm stabbed with pity for him,
but because I have denied my Lord as glaringly as he did. In my

selfishness, by my arrogance, and through my silence, I have denied that Jesus is my Lord. And it hurts to remember. I may not have said the words "I don't know him," but my actions have spoken loudly enough to make it possible to assume. And my inactions in the face of darkness have made it seem apparent that my light was not burning too well in my heart. Every sin I commit, every moment of darkness I allow to pass by without my shedding any light to dispel it is a blatant denial that Jesus is my Lord.

Even though I am not reduced to tears, I can tell that there's something weeping within me. My soul cries out, and it wants to say, "Yes! Yes, I *have* known Him, and I'm His disciple! Come, let me tell you what He's done for me." But then my heart is like Peter's. It just doesn't know the whole picture. It can't understand that every moment of darkness is my moment to shine, my moment of light, and I don't let the light shine.

I am like Peter. Whenever Christ is on trial, I can say that I have followed at a distance—a nice, safe distance. It's safe for me. I just sit by in the courtyard, warming myself by the dark fire of this world, while a spiritual fire within is burning with a longing to set Jesus free. All my heart does is smother those inward flames with fear and self-interested preservation.

And then, like Peter, with the persistent maid telling others, "This man is one of them" (22:58), I am compelled toward the truth of what I have been. My mind sometimes races, wanting to find a way to let Jesus escape from inside of me, while I still don't let Him out. I deny Him the freedom to reach out to others through me, to heal, to speak, to teach, to serve, and to show the way for someone who's lost.

Have you ever felt like Peter? Have you ever become so ashamed of the way you have offended Jesus that it made you weep? What cockcrow shocked you into an awareness of your wrongdoing, of your sinfulness, or of your evil? There are many times in life when we will realize that we've made a mistake. It might be something as obvious as having our humanness exposed, realizing we are fallen, or that there is, in fact, evil within us. Sometimes we can know this only as we see ourselves in the light of Christ. Maybe we can truly discover our wretchedness only by comparison.

Long ago, Jerry Falwell was on *The Phil Donahue Show*. Phil was naturally being antagonistic, questioning the evangelist about the things he said and did. Phil quoted the song "Amazing Grace" with the lyrics, "Amazing grace, how sweet the sound that saved a wretch like me" Then Phil said, "Jerry, I am not a wretch!" I think Phil wanted Jerry to talk about who really needed to be saved. But Jerry said, "You are, compared to Jesus!" And that was exactly what I wanted him to say. When we look at ourselves in the light of Christ, we see our darkness all the more clearly. And we need to, but hopefully not the way Peter did. His denial was totally blatant, perhaps done out of a shallow sense of self-preservation. He feared what might be done to him if he was identified with Christ. But he *was* identified with Christ! Christ was his Lord, his master. How could he deny that? It would be like denying that Tom Kingery is your friend! Even though you might want to, you can't deny the truth. You might admit it while rolling your eyes, which, in its own way, is a sort of denial. But Peter feared the risk. We deny our Lord every time we don't identify ourselves with Him when He comes up in conversation, or when His church is mocked or ridiculed and we should come to its defense. Sometimes, we deny Jesus without really knowing it. We may do so unconsciously.

I don't think Peter *wanted* to deny Jesus. But the maid in the courtyard pushed. She kept pushing until, for Peter, the truth became a threat and something within him went into gear—probably that unconscious overarching sense of self—and the fear of arrest. In his heart, Peter wanted to be loyal, but, "The heart is deceitful above all else; it is perverse—who can understand it?" (Jeremiah 17.9).

Paul explained it this way:

> "I do not understand my own actions. For I do not do what I want, but I do the very thing I hate. Now if I do what I do not want, I agree that the Law is good. But in fact it is no longer I that do it, but sin

that dwells within me. For I know that nothing good dwells within me, that is, in my flesh. I can will what is right, but I cannot do it. For I do not do the good I want, but the evil I do not want is what I do.

"Now, if I do what I do not want, it is no longer I that do it, but sin that dwells within me. So I find it to be a law that when I want to do what is good, evil lies close at hand. For I delight in the Law of God in my inmost self but I see in my members another law at war with the law of my mind, making me captive to the law of sin that dwells in my members. Wretched man that I am! Who will rescue me from this body of death? Thanks be to God through Jesus Christ our Lord!" (Romans 7:15–25)

Thanks be to God through Jesus Christ, our Lord! What we need is less of self and more of Christ. Here's how: "I have been crucified with Christ. It is no longer I who live, but it is Christ who lives in me. And the life I now live in the flesh I live by faith in the Son of God" (Galatians 2:19b–20). We need to die! We need to identify with Jesus in such a way that we can say with Paul, "I have been crucified with Christ!" We need to die to self.

Back to Romans:

If we have been united with Him in a death like His, we will certainly be united with Him in a Resurrection like His. We know that our old self was crucified with Him so that the body of sin might be destroyed, and we might no longer be enslaved to sin. For whoever has died is freed from sin. But if we have died with Christ, we believe that we will also live with Him. We know that Christ, being raised from the dead, will never die again; death no longer has dominion over him. The death He died He died to sin, once for all; but the life He lives, He lives to God. So you also must consider yourselves dead to sin and alive to God in Christ Jesus!" (Romans 6:5–11)

Memorize verse eleven: "Consider yourselves dead to sin and alive to God in Christ Jesus." The more we identify ourselves with Jesus Christ, the more we become united with Him. The more our old selves become crucified with Him, the more we are freed from sin! The more we live a surrendered life, the more the Spirit of Christ will take over. Again, from Romans: "Therefore, do not let sin exercise dominion in your mortal bodies, to make you obey their passions. No longer present your members to sin as instruments of wickedness, but present yourselves to God as those who have been brought from death to life, and present your members to God as instruments of righteousness. For sin will have no dominion over you since you are not under law but under grace" (6:12–14).

A surrendered life is not a morbid life, but a triumphant life. It is a life under grace! Peter had not truly surrendered yet. And even when he did, the triumphant life did not immediately come in its completeness. Peter is speaking from experience when he says,

> Blessed be the God and Father of our Lord Jesus Christ! By His great mercy He has given us a new birth into a living hope through the Resurrection of Jesus Christ from the dead, and into an inheritance that is imperishable, undefiled, and unfading, kept in heaven for you, who are being protected by the power of God through faith for a salvation ready to be revealed in the last time. In this you rejoice, even if, now for a little while, you have had to suffer various trials so that the genuineness of your faith being more precious than gold, that, though perishable, is tested by fire may be found to result in praise and glory and honor when Jesus Christ is revealed! (1 Peter 1:3–7)

Yes, there would still be times of trials in his life, but he knew that by the grace of God, those trials were revealing the genuineness of his own faith.

In His second letter, he said,

> His divine power has given us everything we need for life and godliness, through the knowledge of Him who called us by his own glory and goodness. Thus He has given us, through these things, his precious and very great promises, so that through them you may escape from the corruption that is in the world because of passion, and may become participants of the divine nature. For this very reason, you must make every effort to supplement your faith with goodness, and goodness with knowledge, and knowledge with self-control, and self-control with endurance, and endurance with godliness, and godliness with mutual affection, and mutual affection with love. For if these things are yours and are increasing among you, they keep you from being ineffective and unfruitful in the knowledge of our Lord Jesus Christ. (2 Peter 1:3–8)

Peter knew that the escape from corruption was a process, and that in that process there comes self-control. Only Luke reports the very profound little detail of verse 22:61 in his Gospel. When the cock crowed, "The Lord turned and looked at Peter." I believe it was a look of pity, not of disdain.

What can give you your wake-up call, your call to self-awareness and to the realization that you are not quite the disciple you say you are? And what is the expression on the face of Christ when He turns to look at you?

Don't deny Jesus access to others through you. The cock crows at dawn. Let the sun rise. And let the Son rise!

Mockery

Now the men who were holding Jesus
began to mock him and beat him;
they also blindfolded him and kept asking him,
"Prophesy! Who is it that struck you?"
They kept heaping many other insults on him.
When day came,
the assembly of the elders of the people,
both chief priests and scribes,
gathered together, and they brought him to their council.
They said, "If you are the Messiah, tell us."
He replied, "If I tell you, you will not believe;
and if I question you, you will not answer.
But from now on the Son of Man will be seated
at the right hand of the power of God."
All of them asked, "Are you, then, the Son of God?"
Then he said, "You say that I am."
Then they said, "What further testimony do we need?
We have heard it ourselves from his own lips!"
(Luke 22:63–71)

It seems like the wonderful Hebrew spirit of loving your neighbor as you'd love yourself, the beautiful sense of hospitality that marked the Jewish attitude toward others, the glorious qualities of mercy, holiness, and grace all flew out the window when it came to Jesus, the one God sent to save them from their sins. Jesus was treated as an unscrupulous blasphemer even before He was convicted, even before His formal trial had begun.

That is what upset them the most, though: that He claimed to be the Son of God. In Matthew 26:65 and Mark 14:63, when Jesus indicates that He is the Son of God, the high priest tears his clothes (which was an expression of extreme grief), and says, "He has blasphemed! Do we still need witnesses? Luke doesn't report that they tore their clothes, but he does report them saying something similar: "What further testimony do we need? We have heard it from His own lips" (Luke 22:71). But Jesus had said, "You say that I am" (v. 70).

Let's back up a bit. In Luke 22:63, it says, "The men who were holding Jesus began to mock Him and beat Him." What do you picture? Do you picture Roman soldiers doing this? If you follow Luke carefully, you'll find they're not on stage until they bring Jesus before Pilate. You might expect the godless Romans to treat criminals this way, but Jesus was arrested by "a crowd" (v. 47) that consisted of "the chief priests, the officers of the Temple police, and the elders ..." (v.52). None of these people are Romans. They're all Jews!

Now, In the scene where this mockery begins, I think the chief priests and the elders were probably somewhere else in the house of Caiaphas, consulting with one another, preparing for the assembly that would gather at daybreak. If, however, they are standing nearby, amused, or complicit in this shameful mockery, it reveals all the more grievously how gross is their hypocrisy. Only in Luke is this scene of the mocking of Christ carried out by Jewish guards.

In Matthew, Mark, and John, each of them reports this scene happening in the presence of Romans (Matthew 27:27–30; Mark 15:16–19; John 19:1–3). And it happens at the Praetorium, Pilate's headquarters. In Matthew and Mark, it happens after Jesus has been handed over to Pilate to be crucified. So, what might Luke be trying to say here? Or maybe the question should be, what is he trying not to say? Although he seems to make the Jews look worse, it may make the Romans look less evil. And though it is very difficult to know exactly why Luke reports this episode the way he does, the mockery

Jesus endured is nothing short of evil. It is graceless. It lacks mercy, and it shows a terrible absence of faith in a just God.

Don't you hate bullies? You can't help but feel contempt for anyone who would gang up on someone or push his or her weight around and taunt someone else. Not only that, but in this scene, they beat Jesus and then they blindfold Him and keep hitting Him as they taunt Him, asking Him to prophesy as to who it was that struck Him. And not only that, but they are heaping insulting remarks on Him in the meantime (Luke 22:63–65).

It's just plain horrid that anyone would want to humiliate another human being in this way, and the drama is not over. The scene changes to daylight. The elders, chief priests, and the scribes gather together, and Jesus is brought to their council. In Matthew, Mark, and John, the trial happens through the course of the night. In Matthew and Mark, there are witnesses who are heard. In Luke and John, however, there is no mention of any testimony from any witnesses. In both Luke and John, you get the impression that Jesus is being railroaded—there is no formal trial; a conviction of guilt is all they want, and all they need to do is convince themselves. Even in Matthew and Mark, the trial is a farce. It is a mockery of justice.

In each gospel, the chief priests seem to want Jesus to implicate Himself. They want Him to admit out loud that He is what they fear most. In Matthew, the high priest says, "I put you under oath before the living God, tell us if you are the Son of God" (26:63). In Mark, the high priest says, "Are you the Messiah, the Son of the blessed one?" (14:61). In John, it simply says, "The high priest questioned Jesus about His disciples and about His teaching" (18:19).

But here in Luke, it has the whole Sanhedrin saying, "If you are the Messiah, tell us" (22:67). And after His initial response, Luke reports, "All of them asked, 'Are you, then, the Son of God?'" And this is in response to Jesus having said, "From now on the Son of Man will be seated at the right hand of the power of God" (v. 69). This is a very powerful Messianic image, and it evokes the question, "Are you, then, the Son of God?" Jesus's answer: "You say that I am" (v. 70).

In effect, His words reveal to them that just the fact that they ask the question implies that what they are saying, says it all. It's more like, "What you say says I am!" Note, however, that Jesus said, "I am." If He has said it in Hebrew, which we should assume He does. He is saying, "Yahweh," the name of God, which was never spoken out loud. To do so at the time of Christ was considered blasphemy. It was thought that to speak the name of God was to invoke His presence. To speak it casually or informally was to do so in a disrespectful manner, and thereby to bring on God's wrath.

But this mockery of justice is so ungodly that it would seem to invoke the wrath of God within Jesus's accusers anyway. And guess what! Jesus *is* the presence of God. God's wrath is absent, though, because what is happening is God's mercy. The whole process of this drama is God's plan for salvation. Remember, all the sins of every person, past, present, and future, were poured into Jesus. And Jesus then died for our sins.

Finally, Luke has a wonderful way of establishing the truth. He ends the scene with words that are able to echo in the minds of all who hear them: "What further testimony do we need? We have heard it from His own lips" (v. 71). Indeed! What further testimony do we need? We have heard it from those who've heard it from those who've heard it from His own lips! Jesus had said, though, "If I tell you, you will not believe …" (v. 67b). If I tell you, would you believe? Or would you mock *me*?

I say that Jesus is the Son of God! Jesus is the Messiah, the Christ! Jesus is Lord. I believe it. I trust it, and I proclaim it to you.

The Verdict

Then the assembly rose as a body and brought Jesus before Pilate.
They began to accuse him, saying,
"We found this man perverting our nation,
forbidding us to pay taxes to the emperor,
and saying that he himself is the Messiah, a king."
Then Pilate asked him, "Are you the King of the Jews?"
He answered, "You say so."
Then Pilate said to the chief priests and the crowds,
"I find no basis for an accusation against this man."
But they were insistent and said,
"he stirs up the people by teaching throughout all Judea,
from Galilee where he began even to this place."
When Pilate heard this, he asked whether the man was a Galilean.
And when he learned that he was under Herod's jurisdiction,
he sent him off to Herod,
who was himself in Jerusalem at that time.
When Herod saw Jesus, he was very glad,
for he had been wanting to see him for a long time,
because he had heard about him
and was hoping to see him perform some sign.
He questioned him at some length, but Jesus gave him no answer.
The chief priests and scribes stood by, vehemently accusing him.
Even Herod with his soldiers treated him
with contempt and mocked him;
then he put an elegant robe on him, and sent him back to Pilate.

That same day Herod and Pilate became friends with each other;
before this they had been enemies.
Pilate then called together the chief priests,
the leaders, and the people,
and said to them, "You brought me this man
as one who was perverting the people,
and here I have examined him in your presence
and have not found this man guilty of any
of your charges against him.
Neither has Herod, for he sent him back to us.
Indeed, he has done nothing to deserve death.
I will therefore have him flogged and release him."
Then they all shouted out together,
"Away with this fellow! Release Barabbas for us!"
(This was a man who had been put in prison for an insurrection
that had taken place in the city,
and for murder.)
Pilate, wanting to release Jesus, addressed them again;
but they kept shouting, "Crucify, crucify him!"
A third time he said to them, "Why? What evil has he done?
I have found in him no ground for the sentence of death;
I will therefore have him flogged and then release him."
But they kept urgently demanding with loud shouts that
he should be crucified; and their voices prevailed.
So Pilate gave his verdict that their demand should be granted.
He released the man they asked for,
the one who had been put in prison for insurrection and murder,
and he handed Jesus over as they wished.
(Luke 23:1–25)

Think about some of the things you've been talked into doing. We get talked into doing things by peer pressure: You'll be cool if you smoke—cigarettes or dope. You'll be a real man or woman if you become intimate. Steal this thing and you'll be a hero. Drive really fast, and you'll be cool. Cheat, lie, gossip, drink—don't worry, everybody does. We can get talked into buying some things by salespeople, by advertising, by selfishness, and by lust and desire. Many of the things we let ourselves get talked into doing are usually sinful. Sometimes, we talk ourselves into doing the wrong thing. And sometimes, we can get talked out of doing the right things.

Pilate was talked into a guilty verdict when it came to Jesus. He gave in to the demand of the Jewish leaders. It says, "They kept urgently demanding with loud shouts that He should be crucified … and their voices prevailed" (v. 23). What are the prevailing voices in your life?

The chief priests lied. They misrepresented what Jesus said about paying taxes. What He'd actually said was, "Give to the emperor the things that are the emperor's, and to God the things that are God's" (Matthew 22:21). Initially, Pilate said, "I find no basis for an accusation against this man" (Luke 23:4). "But … they were insistent" (v. 5a). They accused Jesus of stirring up the people from there to Galilee, trying to make it sound like He was rallying comrades for an insurrection (v. 5b).

Pilate saw through them, though. Not wanting to be complicit in what he saw as a petty religious problem and thinking he could pass the problem off on Herod, Pilate sent them to Herod. Only Luke reports this episode. Luke pictures Herod as having been curious about Jesus; He wanted to see Him do something miraculous. But Jesus wouldn't perform for him.

Often, people are like Herod. They want Jesus to do something for them before they will believe. They have unreasonable and incorrect expectations. What should we expect from Jesus today? What should we expect from His church, from His followers, from His teachings, from His grace at work in all of the above? Herod questioned Jesus at some length, but Jesus said nothing to him. He could have simply asked Herod, "What have you heard about me? What do they say I've done? What do they say I've said?" But Herod's attitude was arrogant. His intentions were selfish. His perspective revolved around the thought, *What can you do for me?* When, in matters of faith and justice, grace, and judgment, the real issue should be: whatever is true.

There was an atmosphere of contempt. "The chief priests and scribes stood by, vehemently accusing Jesus" (v. 10), and when Herod got no response from Jesus, the contempt manifested itself in further mockery. Herod put an "elegant robe" on Jesus and sent Him back to Pilate (v. 11). This was sarcasm. There is no grace in sarcasm.

Luke reports something rather curious here. He says that Herod and Pilate became friends that day (v. 12). Though before, they had been at odds, now they would get along. I believe it was probably because Pilate realized Herod felt the same annoyance he did when it came to the chief priests. Sometimes, the enemy of your enemy is your friend. You can hear that annoyance in what Pilate says to them after summoning them together before him: "You brought me this man as one who was perverting the people; and here I have examined Him in your presence and have not found this man guilty of any of your charges against Him. Neither has Herod, for he sent Him back to us. Indeed, He has done nothing to deserve death. I will therefore have Him flogged and release Him."

Pilate wanted to satisfy them by flogging Jesus. He wanted to mock *them* by releasing Him afterward, but they were persistent. Luke doesn't give the explanation of how "you have a custom that I release someone for you at the Passover" (John 18:39; also see Matthew 27:15, Mark 15:6). Luke merely reports that they demanded the release of Barabbas. The idea was that the governor could show grace at the time of Passover. Luke 23:20 reveals that Pilate wanted to release Jesus.

Still, they insisted. "'Why?' Pilate asked. 'What evil has He done I have found in Him no ground for the sentence of death! I will just have Him flogged and then release Him'" (Luke 23:22). That wasn't enough. They wanted Jesus out of the picture. On the other hand, it was God's plan all along that Jesus would die for the sins of creation.

Somewhere in the process, Pilate gave in. In a way, he surrendered himself to become a reluctant pawn in God's plan. There is a blessing in surrender, but not to be a pawn. Jesus was surrendered. All of us are called on to surrender, but in order to be a better servant. We are supposed to die with Christ to live for God. For Pilate, he simply gave in to the demands of the Jewish leaders. "Their voices prevailed" (v. 23). Luke doesn't say that the chief priests stirred up the crowd (Matthew 27:20; Mark 15:11), but Pilate was talked into doing something he really didn't want to do. He could easily have thought that the Crucifixion of Jesus wouldn't matter to him. So he let them have their way. "He released Barabbas, and he handed Jesus over as they wished" (v. 25).

And so He was delivered the verdict of death. It was not fair. There was no justice. Jesus was innocent, but it was my death He died. It was my sin that convicted Him. It was my guilt He carried to the cross. And yours. And yours. And yours. And yours!

The Cross of Simon

As they led him away, they seized a man,
Simon of Cyrene,
who was coming from the country,
and they laid the cross on him, and made him carry it behind Jesus.
(Luke 23:26)

Jeremiah was a man so compelled by the Spirit of God that he couldn't *not* proclaim the prophetic message to the people of his day. He described his calling as a burning in his bones (Jeremiah 20:9). "If I say, 'I will not mention God, or speak any more in His name,' then within me there is something like a burning fire shut up in my bones; I am weary with holding it in, and I cannot!"

Later, Peter and John spoke boldly before the assembly of the elders in Jerusalem. They wanted the two apostles not to speak anymore in the name of Jesus. But Peter and John answered them: "Whether it is right in God's sight to listen to you rather than to God, you must judge; for we cannot keep from speaking about what we have seen and heard" (Acts 4:19–20).

Paul, when he had been blinded at the moment of his conversion, was sent a man named Ananias who, at first, was reluctant to deal with him because of how he had been persecuting the followers of Christ. But Jesus said to him in a vision, "Go, for he is an instrument whom I have chosen to bring my name before Gentiles and kings and before the people of Israel; I myself will show him how much he must suffer for the sake of My name" (Acts 9:15–16).

In many lives, a spiritual calling comes in very deep and powerful ways. It is like a cross to bear. Such a challenge can come upon us the way the cross of Christ came upon Simon on the way to Calvary. He did not choose it. It was laid on him. He was not willing, but he was obedient. He did not resist; he just complied. Christ has said, "If anyone wants to become my followers, let them deny themselves and take up their cross and follow me" (Matthew 16:24). Have you ever heard someone describe a particular burden as their "cross to bear"? It may be a physical impairment of some kind, or it may be the special care they feel obliged to give a loved one with an impairment. Some may describe the jobs they hate as their crosses or relationship they endure. Whatever they may describe as their "crosses," they usually aren't, really.

We, as Christians, are already called upon by Paul to "bear one another's burdens" (Galatians 6:2). "In this way, you will fulfill the law of Christ." The challenges we face are not always crosses. Yes, they may require certain degrees of self-denial. They may come upon us unexpectedly as it did for Simon. But a true cross creates a process of losing your life in order to find it.

The cross of Christ was the means by which He was sacrificed for sin. The cross was where our Lord was crucified. So the cross to be borne by a follower of Christ is not just a personal challenge. It is a spiritual and moral sacrifice by which we die and through which we can be reborn.

The cross we are to bear is the means by which we are able to identify with Christ, and we are to do so in such a way that we can say with Paul, "I have been crucified with Christ. It is no longer I who live, it is Christ who lives in me. And the life I now live in the flesh I live by faith in the Son of God, who loved me; and gave Himself for me" (Galatians 2:20).

In his letter to the Philippians, Paul put it this way: we are to identify with Christ through "sharing His sufferings by becoming like Him in His Death, if somehow I may attain the Resurrection from the dead" (3:10–11). In Galatians, with Paul, we need to have the faith to say, "May I never boast except in the cross of our Lord

Jesus Christ, through which the world has been crucified to me and I to the world" (6:14).

Taking up a cross is not just accepting a challenge of some kind. The cross deals with sin. Our crosses are where we are crucified to the world, and the world to us. The crosses that are imposed on us are our sentences of death. They are the facing of our mortality, of our fallen, sinful natures. The crosses imposed on us are the sacrificial lives that reveal God's redeeming grace and draw us nearer to God. As the great hymn says: "Nearer my God to Thee, nearer to thee; even though it be a cross that raises me" (nineteenth-century Christian hymn by Sarah Flower Adams).

These are imposed on us, for they are imposed on all who believe. They are the message of the cross: "foolishness to those who are perishing, but to us who are being saved it is the power of God" (1 Corinthians 1:18). And when we accept these messages, they become a burning in our bones. We cannot keep from speaking about what we have seen and heard, and we will learn how much we have to suffer for the sake of the name of Jesus.

When these crosses come, obey. Take them up. Deny yourself. Deny your sense of personal gain and follow Christ to Calvary, to judgment, to redemption, to new life, and nearer to God.

When the Wood Is Green

A great number of people followed him,
and among them were women
who were beating their breasts and wailing for him.
But Jesus turned to them and said,
"Daughters of Jerusalem, do not weep for me,
but weep for yourselves and for your children.
For the days are surely coming when they will say,
'Blessed are the barren,
and the wombs that never bore, and the breasts that never nursed.'
Then they will begin to say to the mountains, 'Fall on us';
and to the hills, 'Cover us.'
For if they do this when the wood is green, what
will happen when it is dry?" (Luke 23:27–31)

In the midst of Eden, there once stood the tree of life—beautiful, fruitful, and lush (Genesis 2:9). There was shade and comfort and ease beneath that tree. Even beyond Eden, it was remembered. There was a vision: the righteous are "like trees planted by streams of water, which yield their fruit in its season, and their leaves do not wither" (Psalm 1:3).

When your circumstances become dire, when your pain is excruciating, and when the future looks bleak, a vision that conjures feelings of serenity, though far away, can be encouraging. It can give hope. It can sustain your sanity. The mind of Christ, as He struggled out of the city to Calvary, turned inward or onward or beyond, to what He knew in eternity. In His eternal kingdom, Jesus knew, there was a tree of life.

Perhaps His thoughts traveled there as He made His way. Though Luke doesn't say so, we should imagine that, in the gap between verses twenty-five and twenty-six, Jesus had been scourged. In Matthew, Mark, and John, Pilate has Jesus flogged at the time Barabbas is released. (Matthew 27:26; Mark 15:15; John 19:1) This would have left any man almost too weak to walk. Jesus had been hauled around, taunted, beaten, insulted, and humiliated all through the night. He had not slept since Thursday morning. Exhaustion overwhelmed Him in His human state, but Jesus bore the mind of God. So, on He strove.

Luke never says that Jesus fell on the way to Calvary. Only legend pictures Jesus falling. But for some reason, they seize a man and make him carry the burden of Jesus's cross to Golgotha. In that moment of relief, Jesus was able to feel gratitude for Simon. That may have led Him to think thatit was an act of mercy that was imposed on Simon. Simon obeyed. And in that mercy, and through that obedience, Simon was righteous. The righteous are like trees, shade trees, where there is comfort.

Jesus considered that gracious bit of comfort as His mind thought of trees and maybe of the tree of life. But then, the wailing of the women shocked Him out of that brief moment of reverie. He heard their cries and saw their grief, and He felt the future. If persecution like this was what happened when the righteous Lord was present, what would happen when He's been cut off? If they do this to Jesus, how will it go for His followers? "Weep for yourselves and for your children …" (v. 28). Weep for any who have believed and followed. Weep for all who will inherit the vision of discipleship, "for if they do this when the wood is green …" If they do this to a righteous person—a tree planted by streams of water—"What will happen when it is dry?" (v. 31).

"Do not weep for me; weep for yourselves and for your children. For the days are surely coming when they will say, 'Blessed are the barren'" (v. 29). The deepest grief has often been considered that of a mother's at the loss of her child. In that circumstance, the greater blessing sometimes seems to be never to have given birth in the first place. Jesus is alluding to the horrible suffering He foresaw that would come upon believers in the not-too-distant future, particularly the persecution under Domitian, Nero, and Vespasian, let alone the persecution that Saul first pursued. The fear would be so great that people would just want to hide. "They will say to the mountains, 'Fall on us;' and to the hills, 'Cover us!'" (v. 30).

Think:

How do you hide to avoid being persecuted? When do you choose the blessing with the least amount of risk? Where can we offer mercy? When and how is it sometimes forced upon us the way it was forced on Simon? How will we obey for righteousness' sake? Do we grieve the Crucifixion of Christ … even as we glory in His cross? If Jesus is the green wood, are we the dry wood? How will we do when the fiery ordeal comes upon us? Or are we, who are disciples of Jesus, the green wood of today? What happens when spiritual dryness seems to come upon us? How can we be green wood? Realize that green wood is still growing. What is the vision in your mind that could sustain you with some degree of serenity when your circumstances become dire?

Can you picture the tree of life? Will you harvest its fruit?

Jesus, Remember Me

Two others also, who were criminals,
were led away to be put to death with him.
When they came to the place that is called the skull,
they crucified Jesus there
with the criminals,
one on his right and one on his left.
Then Jesus said,
"Father, forgive them; for they do not know what they are doing."
And they cast lots to divide his clothing.
And the people stood by watching;
but the leaders scoffed at him, saying,
"He saved others;
let him save himself if he is the Messiah of God, his chosen one!"
The soldiers also mocked him, coming
up and offering him sour wine,
and saying, "If you are the King of the Jews, save yourself!"
There was also an inscription over him,
"This is the King of the Jews."
One of the criminals who were hanged there
kept deriding him and saying,
"Are you not the Messiah? Save yourself and us!"
But the other rebuked him, saying,
"Do you not fear God,
since you are under the same sentence of condemnation?
And we indeed have been condemned justly,

for we are getting what we deserve for our deeds,
but this man has done nothing wrong."
Then he said,
"Jesus, remember me when you come into your kingdom."
He replied,
"Truly I tell you, today you will be with me in Paradise."
(Luke 23:32–43)

Take note of people's various attitudes in this scene. Some are the sort I believe Jesus would want to forget. But there is one attitude I believe Jesus would want to—and did—remember. The Crucifixion of Christ cannot be ignored. Everyone has a reaction. The attitude expressed by Jesus is that of unconditional forgiveness. That is the overarching theme of the whole drama. But there are the opposing attitudes of the two others who were crucified beside Him. I will focus on these in a little bit.

First, consider the guards at the foot of the cross who "divided up His clothing by casting lots" (v. 34b). Their attitude reflects the thought, "What can I get from all this for myself?" Behind that, though, is the attitude of doing one's duty—a sort of "doing what you have to do without having to really think about it." However, they would soon join in further mockery, and their commanding officer would eventually express his sense of judgment about Jesus when he says, "Surely this was a righteous man" (v. 47).

Consider next the variety of attitudes among the spectators. Assume that there were people in the crowd grieving over the suffering of their friend and teacher. Some may have felt sorry for Him, the healer, the miracle worker, the good man who was now going to die. Some may have felt confusion and questioned, "Why?" Some people present probably had a morbid attraction to the idea of watching the three men die, wondering who would die first and what each one might say. Maybe they even wondered if the miracle worker would miraculously endure it all and actually save Himself.

Some may have been ready, waiting for a messianic army to appear, rise up, and start the rebellion they wanted to join for the sake of the kingdom of Israel. In the gospel of Matthew, at the moment of Jesus's arrest, when the short fight broke out, Jesus said, "Put your sword back into its place; for all who take the sword will perish by the sword. Do you not know that I can appeal to my Father, and He will send twelve legions of angels?" (26:52–53). There was the assumption that the Messiah would wield this kind of power. But for those who felt this way, the longer they waited and watched, the greater their disappointment may have grown when nothing of the sort happened.

Those closest to Jesus were not too far away, but they looked on in fear, feeling helpless and afraid for themselves. The rulers of the people sneered sarcastically, saying, "He saved others; let Him save Himself if He is the Christ of God, the Chosen One" (v. 35b). Add to this the expression of sarcasm from Pilate with the sign nailed over the head of Jesus that said, "This is the King of the Jews" (v. 38). What reactions do you suppose this elicited from the spectators?

Some might say that there could have been an attitude of justice in what was happening. Surely, that may have been the case with the two criminals. But some may have felt satisfied by the notion that Jesus, the threat to the status quo, was being dealt with in this act of punishment.

Could there have been some who were indifferent? Not at this scene. They are off stage, in the city, going about business as usual. Maybe they just didn't pay attention to anything other than their own little worlds. They may have known something was happening in Jerusalem, but they didn't want to get involved.

And finally, there would have been those who aren't in the scene but who might have cared if they were aware of what was happening. Many people live with hedges around themselves. They are like children: too innocent to be aware yet, or too content to look out their windows. You can't really find fault with them. They just don't know.

Those are all small roles in this scene. The two criminals are the center of attention. They reveal some very important attitudes in the spectrum of this drama. First, there is the angry criminal. Hurling insults at Jesus (v. 39a), he resents Jesus for the simple reason that he thinks Jesus could get him out of this. "Aren't you the Christ? Save

Yourself and us" (v. 39b). He has no respect, no faith. He's saying, "Do something for *me* because you can!" This reflects the extent of belief in many even today. They think that if Jesus is the Savior, He ought to save *me*. It's His job, after all. The attitude is not unlike what you might call foxhole faith. It believes only for the purpose of "get me out of this." It doesn't seek salvation; it only wants rescue. It bears no devotion, but it expects favor. It shows no commitment, but it appeals for mercy. All this criminal really wants is a shortcut, a blanket pardon, but he has no remorse.

In the other criminal, you can hear his remorseful tone: "Don't you fear God? We're all condemned men! We deserve what is happening. But Jesus has done nothing wrong" (vv. 40–41, paraphrased). The faithful believer knows he or she is a sinner. This person knows he or she deserves judgment, but the person places his or her hope in Christ. The second criminal expresses an understanding of Jesus that the chief priests couldn't grasp and that the soldiers just don't see, but that we, the audience—we, the readers—believe without a doubt: Jesus has done nothing wrong!

We are supposed to identify with this man. We are supposed to sympathize with his condition. We deserve punishment, but we want hope. We would not even want to be like the other criminal: arrogant and presumptuous, feeling entitled to whatever he demands, and wanting to exploit the grace of God. We are supposed to want to be humble in our fear of God, remorseful in our judgment, but optimistic in our hope and confident in our trust.

The second criminal does not ask to be rescued. He does not ask for escape. He requests no comfort, no relief. He simply expresses a poverty-ridden faith by begging Jesus, "Remember me when you come into your kingdom" (v. 42). There was no pride, only hope. It is a minimal sort of belief. It is the sort of faith that is just enough. The man was not a follower; he was not a disciple. He did not practice a life of righteousness, since he admitted his punishment was deserved. But Jesus promised him that, "Today you will be with me in Paradise" (v. 43).

By Paradise, Jesus could not have meant death, because the other thief was going to die too, and he was *not* going to be with Jesus in Paradise. The remorseful one who believed in Jesus, would enter the kingdom with Jesus. Jesus's kingdom is Paradise! Now, don't assume that all you have to do before you die is ask Jesus to remember you. This criminal did much more than that. This man rebuked the sinful attitude of the angry criminal. He believed Jesus was the Messiah and that Jesus had a glorious kingdom beyond this world. He may have been guilty of a crime or of sin, but he *did* fear God, and he was remorseful, not defiant. And he believed Jesus was innocent. All that in just three verses! We are meant to identify with him. His request to be remembered expresses trust and confidence as well as humility and hope. How do you want to be remembered? How do you want Jesus to remember you?

At a Distance, Watching

It was now about noon,
and darkness came over the whole land until three in the afternoon,
while the sun's light failed;
and the curtain of the temple was torn in two.
Then Jesus, crying with a loud voice, said,
"Father, into your hands I commend my spirit."
Having said this,
he breathed his last.
When the centurion saw what had taken place, he praised
God and said, "Certainly this man was innocent."
And when all the crowds who had gathered there for this spectacle
saw what had taken place,
they returned home, beating their breasts.
But all his acquaintances,
including the women who had followed him from Galilee,
stood at a distance,
watching these things.
Now there was a good and righteous man named Joseph,
who, though a member of the council,
had not agreed to their plan or action.
He came from the Jewish town of Arimathea,
and he was waiting expectantly for the kingdom of God.
This man went to Pilate and asked for the body of Jesus.
Then he took it down,
wrapped it in a linen cloth,

and laid it in a rock-hewn tomb where no one had ever been laid.
It was the day of Preparation, and the sabbath was beginning.
The women who had come with him from Galilee followed,
and they saw the tomb and how his body was laid.
Then they returned, and prepared spices and ointments.
On the sabbath they rested according to the commandment.
(Luke 23:44–56)

How do you view the Crucifixion of Jesus? Was it a necessary evil? Was it a cruel and unusual punishment? A tragedy? Was it a sacrifice for sin? Was it an act of judgment? A ransom? A substitution? An atonement? A reparation or restitution? A retribution? Was it a means of bringing satisfaction to the devil? Is it payment? At a minimum, it is a story about a man who was willing to suffer and die for what He believed. Scholars have defined it at different times as all of the above.

However we may intellectualize the fact that Jesus was crucified and died, we all have a tendency, at least occasionally, to keep the Crucifixion at a distance. We may welcome the cross as a symbol in our lives, but the Crucifixion is something many would rather forget. It was horrible. It was unjust. It was wrong. But it is the ransom that sets us free from sin and judgment. It was the sacrifice that atoned for our guilt and our fallenness. It was the punishment we deserved but for which Jesus took in our place. He is our substitute. By His wounds, we are healed.

How would you explain the necessity of Jesus's Crucifixion to a non-Christian friend? Paul said, "For our sake God made Him to be sin who knew no sin, so that in Him we might become the righteousness of God" (2 Corinthians 5:21). Paul also said, "The death He died, He died to sin, once for all so you also must consider yourselves dead to sin and alive to God in Christ Jesus" (Romans 6:10–11).

Begin by understanding that nothing that is unholy can enter into God's presence. But God wants us to come to Him, so we have to be made holy! That's why He came to us, to show the way and to *be* the way—as Jesus Christ. We need to become holy, righteous. Something needs to set us right with God, to justify us. The sacrifice of Christ gives us grace, and by that grace we are saved from sin to a right relationship with God if we accept what Jesus has done for us. And *that* makes us holy!

We talk about the Crucifixion even on Maundy Thursday because of the body of Christ that was broken for us and the blood of Christ that was shed for us on the cross. When Jesus told His disciples at His Last Supper to think of the bread and the cup in remembrance of Him, it was a premonition of the Crucifixion.

When the words of institution that bless the elements of communion are said, it is comfortable and sanitary, almost sterilized, as we think only of bread being broken and only of juice being poured into a cup. I think we often tend to think of the remembrance of Christ in our ritual as a remembrance of Jesus as He taught and healed, rather than as He bled and died. When we think of the sacrifice He made on our behalf, all too often, we keep it at a distance.

"When all the people who had gathered to witness this sight saw what took place, they beat their breasts and went away. ... But all those who knew Him, including the women who followed Him from Galilee, stood at a distance, watching these things" (vv. 48–49).

Sometimes it is easier to keep a distance. Sometimes, it is safer. But "The gate is wide and the way is easy that leads to destruction" (Matthew 7:13). By being safe and easy, we won't get any blood on us. It doesn't hurt as much, we think. Joseph of Arimathea didn't play it safe. He took the body of Christ down from the cross, got Christ's blood on his own hands in the process, and buried Him.

Come close. Decide to come close to Christ. Don't play it safe. A cautious faith may feel good, but it does little to transform others or the world. Take to heart the Crucifixion ... the broken body on the cross, the blood that was shed on the cross.

Truly say with Christ, "Father, into your hands I commend my Spirit" (v. 46).

PART IV

The Blood of Christ

Introduction

But what will I get for my sacrifice?

There is no reward that you will see.

Won't I get credit for what I will give?

Why are you so concerned with what you will gain?

I just need a reason for choosing this path.

There is no reason, only sacrifice.

Then why is this called for?

You ask questions that have no simple answers.

But what purpose will it serve?

The purpose is to make a sacrifice. It will serve my purposes.

But why should I want to sacrifice anything?

No one ever wants to make a real sacrifice.

What makes a sacrifice real?

Expecting nothing in return.

Will my sacrifice help someone else?

You are still expecting something.

But what good will it do?

Why must you see more to your sacrifice than just a sacrifice?

Can't I be glad for what I will have accomplished by my suffering?

You'll never know what you accomplish, if anything.

I don't know if I can do it.

It's not a question of whether or not you can, you must!

I don't know how to make a real sacrifice.

You've always expected something, haven't you?

It doesn't make sense to just make a sacrifice without any reason!

You have to have trust.

Will my sacrifice be acceptable?

If it is real.

How can I do it?

I'll be right there with you.

The above dialogue is the type used in ancient Greek theater as an interlude between plays. After an intermission and before the first act of another play, such brief dialogues would serve mainly to silence the crowd and draw their attention. The play that followed this dialogue was probably a drama either about Christ or about one of His teachings.

In my studies, however, I have been compelled to see a separate purpose for these "interludes." I believe they are an entity unto themselves and were also likely to have been read or performed by candidates for baptism, new converts. Such "dialogues" served as a resource for Christian identity and theological exposition.

The dialogue here has been identified for three possible uses. Names are never mentioned, so flexibility of use is possible. Research shows how it could have been used as a dialogue between 1) Abraham and Isaac, 2) between God and Jesus, and 3) between God and the tree from which the cross was cut.

This dialogue leans heavily upon the idea of "giving, expecting nothing in return" as in Luke 6:35—a theme of an unnamed, unknown full-length play. We're meditating on the week of Christ's passion—a time when we honor Christ for the sacrifice that He made on our behalf. It is also a time when we dedicate ourselves to an ever-deeper devotion and when we lift ourselves in faith through the joy of the Resurrection.

It may seem strange to suggest that we can, in some way, celebrate by being sacrificial. But we need equal measures of both celebration and sacrifice, otherwise we fall out of balance theologically and morally. The meditations here are about the blood of Christ. A sacrifice was made that makes us whole. Remember, the sacrifice acceptable to God is a broken spirit (Psalm 51:17).

The following meditations consider those objects in the passion of Christ that had to do with His actual bleeding. Some things caused the bleeding; others got His blood on them. The sacrifice of Christ for my sins included the brutality of my crucifixion. He went through it for me and for you. "Without the shedding of blood there is no forgiveness of sin" (Hebrews 9:22).

It may sound archaic, but realize, "The life of the flesh is in the blood, and I have given it to you for making atonement for your lives on the altar; for as life, it is the blood that makes atonement" (Leviticus 17:11). The Hebrew sacrificial system used animals, shedding their blood to make atonement for guilt and sin. The time of Christ's passion was the Passover, when the lambs were slaughtered at the temple and when Jesus was crucified. His sacrifice as an innocent soul was the perfect sacrifice. "Once for all" (Hebrews 10:10). See that larger passage.

> Since the law has only a shadow of the good things to come, and not the true form of these realities, it can never, by the same sacrifices that are continually offered year after year, make perfect those who approach. Otherwise, would they not the have ceased being offered, since the worshipers, cleansed once for all, would no longer have any consciousness of sin? But in these sacrifices there is a reminder of sin year after year. For it is impossible for the blood of bulls and goats to take away sins. Consequently, when Christ came into the world, he said:

> "Sacrifices and offerings you have not desired, but a body you prepared for me; in burnt offerings and sin offerings you have taken no pleasure. Then I said, 'See, I come to do your will, O God.' (in the scroll of the book it is written of me)." (Hebrews 10:1–10)

When he said above, "You have neither desired nor taken pleasure in sacrifices and offerings, and burnt offerings and sin offerings" (these are offered according to the law), then he added, "See, I have come to do your will" (Psalm 40:6–8). He abolishes the first in order to establish the second. And it is by God's will that we have been sanctified through the offering of the body of Jesus Christ once for all.

Jesus is "the lamb of God who takes away the sin of the world" (John 1:29). His offering, since He was innocent, perfect, and complete, atoning for the sins of the whole world forever. "It is by His wounds [that] we are healed" (Isaiah 53:5, NIV).

The Blood Shed by Christ

He came out and went, as was his custom, to the Mount of Olives;
and the disciples followed him.
When he reached the place, he said to them,
"Pray that you may not come into the time of trial."
Then he withdrew from them about a stone's throw, knelt down,
and prayed, "Father, if you are willing, remove this cup from me;
yet, not my will but yours be done."
Then an angel from heaven appeared to
him and gave him strength.
In his anguish he prayed more earnestly,
and his sweat became like great drops of
blood falling down on the ground.
(Luke 22:39–44)

Working at a zoo, a young man was bitten by a rare and poisonous snake. He was rushed to the hospital. There was a race against time to save him. About an hour and a half away, a man who had a snake farm, whose blood had built up a tolerance to the venom, was contacted. A helicopter would rush him to the hospital where the victim lay, unconscious, his heart slowing down because of the effects of the venom. A transfusion was needed. The patient could be saved only by the blood of the other man. The cure was in the farmer's blood. A life was saved because of it.

Another story: It happened in Vietnam. Two boys, brothers, lived in a village that had been destroyed by the North Vietnamese Army. The older brother was found very badly wounded when the

Americans came in to occupy the territory after the Viet Cong were finally driven out. The boy had lost a lot of blood. After he was stabilized at the mobile hospital, he was still not out of danger. Badly weakened by his blood loss, his body was unable to recover without a transfusion. Because of his blood type, the usual serum was inadequate for his needs. His younger brother was checked and found to be a match. Through a translator, the nine-year-old was told his older brother would die unless he could receive a transfusion. He needed his younger brother's blood.

"Would you be willing to give your blood to save your brother?"

A tear came to the boy's eye. His older brother was protecting him when he was injured. "Yes," he said, "I will give my blood."

There were smiles of relief all around. He was prepared for the procedure, and the transfusion began. It hurt, but the boy knew his blood would save his brother. After about ten minutes, the younger brother began to cry, sobbing and moaning. The nurse stroked his forehead and tried to comfort him, but to no avail. The boy just didn't seem to understand. Finally, the translator was brought in. He asked the boy what was wrong. Was he uncomfortable? Did it hurt? No, the boy said. He was not in pain. He was just so sad. Why? "Because," he began but couldn't go on. Finally, he asked, "When will I die?"

Then the procedure was explained more fully. He would not die at all. He was receiving serum that would sustain his life at the same time that his blood was going into the body of his brother. The crying stopped. At about that time, his brother awakened. His strength was returning, and his life was saved. But the young boy loved his older brother so much that he was willing to die for him, believing simply that all his blood would save his brother's life.

"You know that you were ransomed from the futile ways inherited from your fathers, not with perishable things such as silver and gold, but with the precious blood of Christ" (1 Peter 1:18–19). "In Him we have redemption through His blood, the forgiveness of our trespasses, according to the riches of His grace, which He lavished upon us" (Ephesians 1:7–8). "To Him who loves us and has freed us from our sins by His blood and made us a kingdom, priests to His

God and Father, to Him be glory and dominion for ever and ever. Amen" (Revelation 1:5–6).

I pray that no one feels too uncomfortable hearing about the blood of Christ. In Hebrews 9:22, we are told that "without the shedding of blood, there is no forgiveness of sin." No forgiveness means no salvation. Jesus made the atoning sacrifice that frees us from our fallen nature. He bled and died so we don't have to. Our cure was in His blood! He began to bleed even before He was arrested. The agony of His prayers in the garden of Gethsemane became so intense that he was literally pouring his heart out. Was it blood, or was it sweat pouring out of Him in the same way that blood flows from a gaping wound? The sweat of God, the blood of God Dripping on the ground at the Mount of Olives. The agony of Christ!

But this was only the beginning.

The Whip

Then they took Jesus from Caiaphas to Pilate's headquarters.
It was early in the morning.
They themselves did not enter the headquarters,
so as to avoid ritual defilement
and to be able to eat the Passover.
So Pilate went out to them and said,
"What accusation do you bring against this man?"
They answered,
"If this man were not a criminal. we would not have handed
him over to you." Pilate said to them, "Take him yourselves
and judge him according to your law." The Jews replied,
"We are not permitted to put anyone to death."
(This was to fulfill what Jesus had said
when he indicated the kind of death he was to die.)
Then Pilate entered the headquarters again,
summoned Jesus and asked him,
"Are you the King of the Jews?"
Jesus answered,
"Do you ask this on your own, or did others tell you about me?"
Pilate replied, "I am not a Jew, am I?
Your own nation and the chief priests have handed you over to me.
What have you done?"
Jesus answered,
"My kingdom is not from this world.
If my kingdom were from the world,

my followers would be fighting to keep me from being handed
over to the Jews. But as it is, my kingdom is not from here."
Pilate asked him, "So you are a king?"
Jesus answered,
"You say that I am a king.
For this I was born, and for this I came into the world, to testify to
the truth. Everyone who belongs to the truth listens to my voice."
Pilate asked him,
"What is truth?"
After he had said this, he went out to the Jews again and told them,
"I find no case against him.
But you have a custom that I release
someone for you at the Passover.
Do you want me to release for you the King of the Jews?"
They shouted in reply, "Not this man, but Barabbas!"
Now Barabbas was a bandit.
Then Pilate took Jesus and had him flogged.
(John 18:28–19:1)

In the midst of his agony, as Jesus prayed so intensely in the garden of
Gethsemane that His sweat became like great drops of blood falling
to the ground, a band of soldiers guided by Judas was approaching. In
the gospel of John, when the soldiers arrive, it says, "Jesus, knowing
all that was to befall Him, came forward and said to them, 'Whom
do you seek?' They answered Him, 'Jesus of Nazareth.' Jesus said to
them, 'I am He.'" And, it says that "they drew back and fell to the
ground" (John 18:4–7). Why was there such a shocked reaction?
Jesus was soaked with sweat. He may have been either extremely
flushed or extremely pale from sweating so much. Did He look as
though He was the walking dead? Were they shocked simply because
His surrender was so effortless? Or were they shocked to hear Him
say a word that was too holy to speak? If He spoke in Hebrew, the
statement "I am" is the very name of God, *Yahweh*. It could have been
a combination of all of this.

After a brief scuffle attempted by Simon Peter that Jesus Himself halted, Jesus is seized and bound, taken to the high priest's house for a quick trial, and then led off to the praetorium, to Pontius Pilate. There is no trip to Herod in the gospel of John; that is only in Luke. It is almost as if Pilate is alone with Jesus. Pilate himself moves back and forth between Jesus and the Jews, as they are called in the gospel of John. Pilate examined Jesus briefly by simply asking, "What have you done?" (18:35). And being told by Christ that His kingship was not of this world (v. 36), Pilate comes close to accusing Jesus of trying to be a king. But Jesus says something very cryptic to Pilate: "You say that I am a king. For this I was born, and for this I have come into the world, to bear witness to the truth. Everyone who is of the truth hears my voice" (John 18:37). At that, Pilate sarcastically says, "What is truth?" (v. 38).

You see, from Pilate's point of view, power is truth. The one who has the power possesses the truth. Jesus is a nothing as far as Pilate is concerned. The petty people of Jerusalem are nothing in a vassal state under the all-consuming power of mighty Rome! You know it, and I know it, that the ultimate power actually resides in God, in faith, and in the truth that reveals the kingdom of God. But as far as Pilate is concerned, he is being annoyed. And yet, behind every cynical attitude that outwardly mocks the relevance of faith, the words of derision echo back their deeper sense, and soon enough, Pilate will hear in his own mind his words come back to him as, "What is truth?"

He tells the Jews, "I find no case against Him" (v. 38b). Pilate tries to appeal to a custom that was apparently established and practiced by the Roman governor at previous Passovers, of releasing one prisoner in recognition of Pharoah's release of the Hebrews after the first Passover. But Pilate has contempt for these people of "faith," and he infuriates them by asking if they would have him release "the king of the Jews" (v. 39). It was precisely because the Pharisees saw Jesus claiming to be their "anointed messiah" or "king" that they so objected to Him. Pilate may have known about the popular favoritism Jesus had gained among the common people when He entered the Holy City only the previous Sunday. Perhaps it is to this that he is appealing. However, it was a frail effort at diplomacy because they ask for Barabbas instead. Why they do is another story altogether.

The next thing that happens is that Pilate had Jesus scourged (John 19:1). William Barclay explained, "When a man was scourged, he was tied to a whipping post in such a way that his back was fully exposed. The lash had several long leather thongs, studded at intervals with pellets of lead and sharpened pieces of bone. It literally tore a man's back into strips. Few remained conscious throughout the ordeal; some died, and many went raving mad" (*The Gospel of John, Vol. 2*, p. 244).

Some scholars explain that a scourging was called forty lashes, but only thirty-nine were inflicted because it was claimed that forty could kill a man. The purpose was not death, but punishment. Sometimes, because the process was so horrifying, two men with whips would alternate inflicting the blows, partly so as not to wear out a single man. Some scholars have even imagined the whip as having more than a single thong (e.g., the nine-tails). And if it was done by two men, the man tied to the whipping post would have no time to brace himself for the next blow. Inasmuch as we would react to the oncoming blow by either bracing ourselves, or by pulling away from the infliction of something so painful, imagine not just one or two whacks of a whip, each one able to tear and lacerate your flesh to ribbons, but thirty-nine!

People stood back. Not just to give room to the floggers, but because of the blood that would splatter and the flesh that would occasionally fly off, torn away from the prisoner's back by the blows of the whip, turning a man's back into what would have looked like flailed, raw meat. Those were muscles, battered, bruised, torn. It was more than just His skin that would have hurt; he felt agony in every lacerated muscle of His back. He would have ached beyond any back pain we might imagine. Certainly, the men inflicting the punishment felt blood spattering on them. The whips, when the scourging was done, would have been covered with blood. And, of course, the bleeding would not have stopped when the scourging was complete. It would have flowed unchecked by the protective tissue of the skin, for it, too, would have been shredded into uselessness.

My Savior took this for me. It is sickening to think of what happened to Him, not just because of the excruciating pain He would have endured, but because He didn't deserve it. I did. You did. We did. Certainly, I would rather take the scourging than the everlasting fires of death. But I will receive neither, nor will you, if you accept His suffering for your sin. *His* blood was shed; *He* felt the pain; *He* drew the curse upon Himself that we might be set free, like Barabbas!

Dear Jesus, we know how much you suffered even before you bore your cross. We want to believe your scourging would have been enough. But the weight of the sins of the world must have needed every drop of your precious blood, every cell of your human, life-sustaining substance must have been required to atone for our evils. And because what happened to you was so evil, we feel pain in our hearts knowing it is what we otherwise might deserve. And we thank you for taking our place at the whipping post. Give us grace to sin no more, if only to honor the blood you shed to make us whole. By your holy Spirit we pray, amen.

The Crown of Thorns

And the soldiers wove a crown of thorns and put it on his head.
(John 19:2a)

Jesus Christ is king. He shall reign for ever and ever. His kingdom is not of this world, but He reigns over my life. All the kingdoms of this world will pass away, but His shall be an everlasting kingdom. A time will come when the kingdoms of this world will have become the kingdom of our Lord, and He shall truly reign for ever and ever. And if He is in fact your king, if He truly rules over your life, if you are subject to His will, you will live in His kingdom in eternal life beyond this life. You will have life everlasting, life abundant and life that is life, indeed.

Jesus preached about the kingdom of God. It is like a mustard seed (Matthew 13:31). It is like a merchant in search of fine pearls (13:45–46). It is like treasure hidden in a field (13:44). It is like a little leaven (13:33). It is like a great net that gathers all fish (v. 47). It should be the very thing that, along with righteousness, we should seek first in our lives. And it is like seeds spread by a sower. Some seeds fall among the thorns, and the thorns choke the seeds when they begin to grow (13:7). The thorns are an enemy of the kingdom. They bring pain, while God's kingdom brings peace. The thorns draw blood, while God's kingdom brings healing. The thorns are problems to avoid while the kingdom is promises to keep. The thorns are ugly, but God's kingdom is beautiful. The thorns are a sign of the imperfections of this world, and the kingdom of God is constantly penetrating into this world, leaving its traces of perfect joy, love, and grace.

The thorns are not worth saving. They will be gathered and burned. But in God's kingdom, Jesus Christ is the Savior, gathering His followers, His believers—all who come to Him, having prepared a place for them in His Father's house (John 14:2–3). He is saving them and seeking to save even those who are lost. As for those who are to be citizens of God's kingdom, "You will know them by their fruits. Are grapes gathered from thorns or figs from thistles? So every sound tree bears good fruit, but the bad tree bears evil fruit" (Matthew 7:16–17). In the letter to the Hebrews, we are told,

> It is impossible to restore again to repentance those who have once been enlightened, and have tasted the heavenly gift, and have shared in the Holy Spirit, and have tasted the goodness of the word of God and the powers of the age to come, and then have fallen away, since on their own they are crucifying again the Son of God, and are holding Him up to contempt. Ground that drinks up the rain falling on it repeatedly, and that produces a crop useful to those for whom it is cultivated, receives a blessing from God. But if it produces thorns and thistles, it is worthless and on the verge of being cursed; its end is to be burned over. (Hebrews 6:4–8)

Thorns are a symbol of evil. A crown of thorns was plaited and placed on our Savior's head, piercing the skin of His brow. The hair of His temples, already matted with sweat, would have become matted with blood. Sick and dizzy with pain after His scourging, He was mocked by a host of Romans. One of the men (I wonder if *his* fingers were pricked as he did it) wove a thorny branch of briars into a circle, resembling a crown, and placed it on the head of Christ. The stabbing of its points would have made Him wince. Blood may easily have trickled down His bowed head, over His eyebrows, and into

His eyes, dimming His vision that was likely already blurred by the His pouring sweat. The defiance of their contempt for Christ brings revulsion to my heart. My Savior was mocked! And they laughed.

How do you feel when you are harassed? How do you feel when you see someone being harassed? Most of us can probably recall times in our childhoods when we saw bullies tormenting other children, who, through no fault of their own, were just not as capable, or just not as typical as the average children their age. The taunts, the teasing, the irritating jibes that are directed at such children are not primarily meant to be humiliating. Their first purpose is more like that of subordination. To cut someone else down is to build oneself up, in a sick sort of way. But, as often as not, the people who bully and harass others are even more insecure than those they pick on. The feeling I usually get when I see someone being harassed is an overwhelming desire to put the bullies in their place and to do the exact same thing to them that they are doing to the underdog.

I can remember my sixth grade year when I entered junior high. Kids from two different grade schools were mixed together, similar to what happens in many towns. There were kids I never knew who started picking on one kid I had known for years. When I started to defend him by telling those guys to leave him alone, they started to pick on me too. I want to say that was their mistake, but it was at that point that I began to make the mistake. I stooped to their level and, with whatever sharpness of wit I could summons, God forgive me, I began to return their taunts with insults they just could not appreciate for some reason. So they beat me up.

When the teacher came to break up the fight, I was on top of one guy, trying to push the other guys away, who were trying to stop me from hitting him. Basically, it was three against one. The teacher heard their story before she heard mine, and their story didn't have anything to do with them picking on Pete. Guess who got in trouble. Me! I suppose the moral of the story is that you can't always put someone in his or her place by putting yourself in that person's place and giving that person a taste of his or her own medicine.

Jesus was taunted. He was mocked. He was tormented, harassed, and bullied. After being weakened by the scourging, it seems absurd and senseless to carry on any further. But apparently, the Romans practiced such extraordinary humiliation where others could see it to instill the deepest fear of doing anything that would evoke such consequences on oneself. A condemned person did not merely receive the punishment that was due; he or she was also tortured, humiliated, and cut down to nothing. The person suffered not only physical pain but moral and emotional pain. But after a point, the person's sin isn't just an example of fallen human nature. It is downright evil.

Wanting to degrade someone to the point of humiliation is wrong in the first place. Taking it to extremes is only going to provoke an anger that wants to retaliate somehow. I'd be surprised if there were any of you who were unaware of the incidents of police brutality involving Rodney King that occurred in Los Angeles (It seems so long ago now.). Knowing such brutality occurs leaves a lump in my gut. Seeing it caught on video turns that lump quite sour.

I wanted to retaliate. No matter how wrong the man was, he didn't deserve to be beaten when he was already down. We get angered not only by this type of grotesque meanness, but by the incredible lack of compassion. The idea of showing no mercy sure sounds tough, but the thought of no mercy sounds evil. The lack of kindness in such an attitude is more humiliating to the abuser than the torment is to the one being persecuted.

It is the falseness that is self-abasing. And the reason there is a falseness is that those who dish it out do not want to receive it themselves. It contradicts the most basic principle of humaneness: that of doing unto others what you would have others do unto you. I believe the crown of thorns is perhaps the best symbol for a lack of humaneness and a lack of heart.

The crown of thorns is the exact opposite of what Jesus truly deserves. The crown of thorns gives pain to the one who brought healing. It shows hatred for one who taught love. It shows violence to the one who brought peace. It shows no grace to the one who came by grace to save. It shows no mercy to the merciful Lord who was dying for the sins even of those who were tormenting him.

The crown of thorns sheds blood into the eyes of one who gives his own blood as a gift to the world. It shows laughter at his tears that are mixed with blood. And every thorn, like a person sinning, pierces the mind of the innocent one, who takes that sin upon Himself. And because the crown is made of thorns, it's felt a hundred times a second. Reed or not, it was like a hammer when the guard struck His head, fiercely pounding the points of each thorn into His skull.

I wonder about the one who plaited the crown together. Was he so spartan that he could simply ignore his own pain? Was his skin left unpierced? Did he feel no hurt? I believe his cruel deed would have hurt him. Whether he was indifferent to his own pain or not, he should have known something was wrong. His own blood from his own fingers was shed before the crown brought pain to Christ. But then, there is their crowning shame: they pretended to pay Christ homage. They falsely humbled themselves before God, but to them, he was not God. Their sarcasm is mockery, and ironically, they are only mocking themselves. Their scoffing is their own ridicule. Their ignorance is a caricature of the civilized sophistication the Romans thought they had achieved, but their brutality is our brutality. Their ignorance is our ignorance.

We defend ourselves by saying there is a difference, but it is only in degree. Our brutality is different; we've cleaned it up, and yet, we've distanced ourselves from the pain of others. We are anesthetized to our own hurts, and so we've become indifferent to the hurts of others. Our indifference is humiliating. It is a mockery of our faith. It is contempt when it should be conquered. Because more than anything else, it is our claim to faith that is rendered false by our indifference. Our indifference becomes indifference to Christ. And just as you cannot help but feel compassion for the child tormented by bullies, you should feel no less than love for Jesus. If not because He is good and because He is God, then we should love Him because He has suffered so much. He suffered so much because He loved us so well.

But humanity regards that dark, dirty scene and does not join in the laughter. Humanity falls silent and stands very still. Though unable to alter that hour of deep disrespect, humankind looks with disdain on Christ's mockers. Wishing to come to His aid but paralyzed by the shock of such total disregard for its Savior, humanity is a victim of the same shame He is suffering, while at the same time, humanity is propagating that suffering by its sin. Every sin we commit is like a thorn in that crown. Every act of willful disobedience adds to the scorn of the beaten redeemer. Every time we fail to correct evil, we mock the good. And for every moment that passes or that fails to proclaim the kingdom of God and the reign of Christ, a moment is spent twisting the branch again, shaping it into a crown, pricking the fingers of humanity as it does, and delivering the needle-like thorns into the brow of God in Christ Jesus.

Oh, how our worship is a mockery when we claim no redemption for the world. Oh, how our prayers are so scornful as we seek our own benefits in some shallow sense of wish-fulfillment. Oh, how our lives reveal so great a disregard as to allow what our Savior endured to have little meaning for us!

For as the blood dripped into the eyes of Christ, He became blinded that we might see the grace of His suffering. And as the blood trickled into His ears, He became deafened that we might hear the good news of His perfect sacrifice. And as the taste of His own blood reached His tongue, He remained mute that we might give voice to the love of God revealed in the hour of Christ's substitution for us. What a glorious redemption we have. What a gracious redeemer!

Yet, humanity still looks on. But some, with hearts that ache for the master, whose conscience is pricked by the pain of the thorns and whose compassionate sensibilities are sent surging by the horror of the scene, are compelled to care for the beaten man with a love that would change it all if only it could.

Our king has cast off His divinity to bear the curse of sin. Our king has left His throne to take the pain of our punishment here below. Our king did not count equality with God a thing to be grasped onto. He set aside His crown of glory to wear the crown of thorns and to receive the scorn of shameful sin, to be mocked by a world that respects nothing of honor. Our king bore our disgrace. He was mercilessly humiliated to make us humble, abased to bring us dignity, reproached to bring us respectability. He bled to bring us mercy. The crown of thorns, a sign of all that Christ does not deserve, brought blood from the head that is our Head, cutting into His skin to mock His reign, His kingdom. His love is now evoking in us, who follow in His steps, a gratitude for the true crown that He now wears as we crown Him Lord of all! Think about the crown of thorns. Think about the king. Oh, what a wondrous love!

Almighty God, you suffered scornful humiliation at the hands of humanity, who produced the evil fruit of your suffering. It is we who deserve that gross disregard, for you were innocent. We are guilty, and yet you suffered. We are shameful. You are to be honored. We accept the love you have offered by your sacrifice of self that we might be set free. You have given us a crown. Let us never, never take it for granted. We are enabled to love because you first loved us. Help us to see your love, your holy, perfect love in the things you suffered for our sake. Help us to see it, Lord. In Jesus's name we pray, amen.

The Purple Robe

And they dressed him in a purple robe.
They kept coming up to him, saying, "Hail, King of the Jews!"
and striking him on the face.
Pilate went out again and said to them,
"Look, I am bringing him out to you to let you know
that I find no case against him."
So Jesus came out, wearing the crown of
thorns and the purple robe.
Pilate said to them,
"Here is the man!"
When the chief priests and the police saw him,
they shouted, "Crucify him! Crucify him!"
Pilate said to them, "Take him yourselves and crucify him;
I find no case against him."
The Jews answered him,
"We have a law, and according to that law he ought to die
because he has claimed to be the Son of God."
Now when Pilate heard this, he was more afraid than ever.
He entered his headquarters again and asked Jesus,
"Where are you from?"
But Jesus gave him no answer.
Pilate therefore said to him,
"Do you refuse to speak to me?
Do you not know that I have power to release you,
and power to crucify you?" Jesus answered him,

"You would have no power over me unless it had
been given you from above; therefore the one who
handed me over to you is guilty of a greater sin."
From then on Pilate tried to release him,
but the Jews cried out,
"If you release this man, you are no friend of the emperor.
Everyone who claims to be a king sets
himself against the emperor."
When Pilate heard these words, he brought Jesus outside
and sat on the judge's bench
at a place called the Stone Pavement, or in Hebrew, Gabbatha.
Now it was the day of Preparation for the Passover;
and it was about noon.
He said to the Jews,
"Here is your King!"
They cried out, "Away with him! Away with him! Crucify him!"
Pilate asked them, "Shall I crucify your King?"
The chief priests answered, "We have no king but the emperor."
Then he handed him over to be crucified.
(John 19:2b–16)

Psalm 93:1 begins by proclaiming, "The Lord reigns; He is robed in majesty! The Lord is robed, He is girded with strength." In Psalm 104:1, it says, "Bless the Lord, O my soul! O Lord my God, Thou art very great! Thou art clothed with honor and majesty!"

Jesus taught that we should never be anxious about clothing (Matthew 6:28–30): "Consider the lilies of the field, how they grow; they neither toil nor spin; yet I tell you, even Solomon in all his glory was not arrayed like one of these. But if God so clothes the grass of the field, which today is alive and tomorrow is thrown into the oven, will He not much more clothe you, O men of little faith?" Jesus even taught that should we see the naked, we should clothe them (Matthew 25:36).

And in the all-consuming vision of our faith, where the victory of Christ is pictured, it says,

> Then I saw heaven opened, and behold, a white horse! He who sat upon it is called Faithful and True, and in righteousness He judges and makes war. His eyes are like a flame of fire, and on His head are many diadems; and He has a name inscribed which no one knows but Himself. He is clad in a robe dipped in blood, and the name by which He is called is The Word of God. And the armies of heaven, arrayed in fine linen, white and pure, followed Him on white horses! On His robe and on His thigh, he has a name inscribed: King of kings and Lord of lords. (Revelation 19:11–16)

White is the symbol of victory. But notice how our victorious king wears a robe dipped in or sprinkled with blood. In the gospel of John, the soldiers array Jesus in a purple robe. In Mark 15:17, it is described as a purple cloak. In Matthew 27:28, it is a scarlet robe! And in Luke 23:1, it is described as "glorious apparel," and it is placed on Christ by Herod's soldiers.

In the splendor my Lord shared with God before His incarnation, Jesus was clothed with honor and majesty. On the last day of His earthly life, Jesus was clothed with dishonor and shame. The robe covered the wounds of Christ's scourging. It would have soaked up some of the blood flowing from His wounded back, and it may have been placed upon Him to cover the nauseating hideous mass of flesh on His naked back. As much as you or I would cringe the moment we would clothe ourselves if we were just sunburned, imagine the pain of a heavy robe drawn across those open sores. Jesus is again made to feel the chastisement that makes us whole, the painful stripes by which we are healed.

And to add insult to injury, He is taunted, mockingly hailed as "King of the Jews." The soldiers slap Him around. They punch Him (John 19:3). In Matthew and Mark, they even spit on Him. Meanwhile, Pilate, pretending to be a diplomat, comes out to where the Jewish leaders are waiting and says he finds no crime in Jesus.

Jesus is led out behind Pilate, wearing the crown of thorns and the purple robe. I imagine the contemptuous gesture Pilate performed by pulling the collar of the robe down to expose Christ's bleeding wounds before the people as he says, "Here is the man" (v. 5).

All the more enraged, the chief priests and officers cry out, "Crucify Him! Crucify Him" (v. 6). By this time, Pilate really has the crowd stirred up, and he says, "Take Him yourself and crucify Him, for I find no crime in Him" (v. 6b). But the bloodthirsty Jewish leaders appeal to their own laws, perhaps even the first commandment of having no other gods, and they say, "We have a law, and by that law He ought to die, because He has made Himself the Son of God" (v. 7).

Hearing that scared Pilate. "Where are You from?" he asked Jesus (vv. 8–9). Then, frustrated by Jesus's silence, he tells Him that it is within his power to release Him or to have Him crucified (v. 10). The mockery continues as a mockery of justice. Pilate is just a pawn in this picture. Jesus even tells him that the only power Pilate has is from the institution of his office. He has no power in himself other than from the responsibility placed in his hands. He will not be at fault, Jesus says, "the one who handed me over to you is guilty of a greater sin" (v. 11).

Upon this, Pilate sought to release Him (v. 12). Somehow, he was convinced that Jesus did not deserve what was happening. But realize that Pilate has probably been in this position dozens of times. Other accused men, scourged and beaten, would probably have been before him at this very spot, perhaps daily. They may have been too weak to say anything. If they had any strength at all, they would either be crying for mercy or in a fit of rage, both of which Pilate would have returned with contempt. But no one like Jesus had ever stood before him: clear-minded, rational, even relevant, challenging Pilate's better sensibilities. Not whimpering or belligerent, only righteous and honest. His last attempt to release Jesus came perhaps as a last-ditch effort not to have to release Barabbas. But his effort at graciousness was met with the threat of blackmail: "If you release this man, you are no friend of the emperor. Everyone who claims to be a king sets himself against the emperor" (v. 12b). Good point.

Pilate's last act in this scene is a final expression of contempt. He knows it is a no-win situation. So, as he sits on the formal seat of judgment, he says to the Jewish leaders, "Here is your King" (v. 14b). "Away with Him! Away with Him! Crucify Him" (v. 15a), they cry, angry with Pilate, playing tit for tat with contempt. They would never allow Pilate to get what he wanted in that fateful moment. One last time, he says, "Shall I crucify your King?" (v. 15b). With a final expression of disregard for Pilate's desire to show favor to Jesus, and with an expression of apostasy, for the Jews were supposed to have no king but God, these Jewish leaders are heard to say, "We have no king but the emperor" (v. 15c). At that, Pilate gave in to the pressure. He handed Jesus over to be crucified (v. 16).

Later, while suffering on the cross, the four soldiers who were charged with the Crucifixion, took His garments and divided them, gambling only for the seamless tunic Christ had worn (John 19:23–24). But who would want such bloody clothes? Or had Jesus been wearing them at all? It is likely they had been removed before His scourging and were not bloody at all. But what value could they possibly possess for these soldiers? Ignorant of the power in the blood, they are only pawns, as is Pilate, in the purposes of God. What they do is more than just a matter of getting what they can from the condemned man; they are fulfilling images of prophecy. They remain unnamed and insignificant, only examples of the world's indifference to the suffering criminals. Still, somehow, it is possible to see in them a sense of having something to gain at Christ's expense. And in that regard, they are us.

How indifferent we become to the blood of Christ when it is cold in His garments after the cross has raised Him naked to the world as a condemned man. Today, we see Him robed in majesty and honor and power and glory. But the reason we can see Him this way is because, for one hour of His life, He was arrayed in a purple robe. The robe that covered His wounds.

How are you arrayed? "Clothe yourself with the new nature" (Colossians 3:10).

As God's chosen ones, holy and beloved, clothe yourselves with compassion, kindness, humility, meekness, and patience. Bearing with one another and, if anyone has a complaint against another, forgive each other; just as the Lord has forgiven you, so you also must forgive. Above all, clothe yourselves with love, which binds everything together in perfect harmony. And let the peace of Christ rule in your hearts, to which indeed you were called in the one body. And be thankful. Let the word of Christ dwell in you richly; teach and admonish one another in all wisdom; and with gratitude in your hearts sing psalms, hymns, and spiritual songs to God. And whatever you do, in word or deed, do everything in the name of the Lord Jesus, giving thanks to God the Father through Him. (Colossians 3:12–17)

In Ephesians 6:11, we are told, "Put on the whole armor of God, so that you may be able to stand against the wiles of the devil." Ephesians 6:14–17 says, "Stand, therefore, and fasten the belt of truth around your waist, and put on the breastplate of righteousness. As shoes for your feet put on whatever will make you ready to proclaim the gospel of peace. With all of these, take the shield of faith, with which you will be able to quench all the flaming arrows of the evil one. Take the helmet of salvation, and the sword of the Spirit, which is the word of God."

Put on the power of Christ, and Christ will put a white robe on you—a robe washed in the blood of the lamb! You see, there is power in the blood!

Blood on the Cross

Carrying the cross by himself,
he went out to what is called the place of the skull,
which, in Hebrew, is called
Golgotha.
(John 19:17)

Let me begin with a list of scripture passages.

- "The Son of Man also came not to be served, but to serve, and to give His life as a ransom for many" (Mark 10:45).
- "In Christ God was reconciling the world to Himself, not counting their trespasses against them, and entrusting to us the message of reconciliation" (2 Corinthians 5:19).
- "We preach Christ crucified, a stumbling block to the Jews and folly to the Gentiles, but to those who are called, both Jews and Greeks, Christ is the power of God and the wisdom of God" (1 Corinthians 1:23–24).
- "When I came to you, brothers and sisters, I did not come proclaiming to you the testimony of God in lofty words or wisdom. For I decided to know nothing among you except Jesus Christ and Him crucified" (1 Corinthians 2:1–2).
- "Far be it from me to glory except in the cross of our Lord Jesus, by which the world has been crucified to me, and I to the world" (Galatians 6:14).
- "I have been crucified with Christ; it is no longer I who live, but Christ who lives in me; and the life I now live in the flesh

I live by faith in the Son of God, who loved me and gave Himself for me" (Galatians 2:20).

- "If anyone would come after me, let them deny themselves and take up a cross and follow me" (Matthew 16:24).
- "In Jesus all the fullness of God was pleased to dwell, and through Him to reconcile to Himself all things, whether on earth or in heaven, making peace by the blood of His cross" (Colossians 1:19–20).
- "Now is the judgment of this world; now shall the ruler of this world be cast out; and I, when I am lifted up from the earth, will draw all people to myself" (John 12:31–32).
- "As Moses lifted up the serpent in the wilderness, so must the Son of Man be lifted up, that whoever believes in Him may have eternal life" (John 3:14–15).

The cross is a symbol of power, for there is power in our belief if we believe that Jesus's death on the cross is our salvation. The cross is a symbol of belief because of our very dependence on what happened there for our salvation. Each of us is able to say that the cross is a symbol of *my* death because Christ died for *me*. We can also say that the cross is a symbol of the death of our sins because the suffering and punishment Christ received is on our behalf.

The cross is a symbol of death's defeat, for the cross is now empty, and so is the grave. The cross is a symbol of power over evil, as in the mythical image of it being used in fictional stories to chase away demons and defend against vampires. The cross is a symbol of the death of selfishness, as we are called through our discipleship to deny ourselves, take up a cross, follow the example of Christ, and to make sacrifices for the sake of others.

The cross is a symbol of grace because Jesus gave His life to give us the free gift of forgiveness. It is a symbol of forgiveness and reconciliation because at the cross is where Jesus ransomed us. It is also a symbol of love because God so loved the world that He gave His only Son. The cross is a symbol of judgment because "those who believe in Jesus are not condemned; but those who do not believe are condemned already, because they have not believed in the name of the only Son of God" (John 3:18). It is also a symbol of faith because of our trust in this grand act of reconciliation!

Scourged and beaten, Jesus is then forced to bear His cross, or, at least, the crossbeam, from the Praetorium to Golgotha—the place of the skull (John 19:17). We often picture something almost the size of a railroad tie, the weight of a hundred pounds or so, but that is very unlikely. It would have been a waste of good timber. Something more practical would have been a minimal board, which was big enough to hold only a man's weight suspended indefinitely as he suffered.

The upright post would have been sturdier. And although I prefer to envision a fully made cross dragged up the trail of tears to Calvary, outside the city walls, the Romans were far more practical than to stack crosses at the praetorium, and the impossibility of a beaten man carrying so much weight for such a great distance (two blocks or so), makes it reasonable to think that the post was already at the execution site.

The crossbeam would have been laid across Christ's wounded shoulders. It is also likely that his arms would have been tied onto it, as some portrayals reveal. Matthew and Mark say that the soldiers put Christ's own clothes on Him before they led Him out to be crucified (Matthew 27:31; Mark 15:20). But nowhere do the gospels ever say that Jesus fell along the way. In Matthew, Mark, and Luke, a man named Simon from Cyrene (in Mark 15:21, it is even explained that he is the father of Alexander and Rufus!), from a part of North Africa, was compelled to carry the cross for Christ (Matthew 27:32, Mark 15:21, Luke 23:26). Did he get any blood on himself? I bet he did!

Certainly, the post of the cross would have become bloody. This is when Jesus was stripped, and He was laid on His back on the wood. The pain would have been unbearable. Remember, His back had received the thirty-nine blows of the whip's lashes, and the thongs of the whip had bits of lead and sharpened bones in their tails. His back had been ripped and shredded. Now, if the blood flow had slowed, it would have been pouring again. And it would get worse.

The soldiers charged with this act of execution probably wouldn't have cared, but some in the crowd that followed along the way to Golgotha did. In Luke, a group of women were wailing and lamenting Him (Luke 23:27–31), but Jesus told them not to weep for Him. "Weep for yourselves and for your children. For behold, the days are coming when they will say, 'Blessed are the barren, and the wombs that never bore, and the breasts that never gave suck!' Then they will begin to say to the mountains, 'Fall on us'; and to the hills, 'Cover us.' For if they do this when the wood is green, what will happen when it is dry?" If the fire of hades is consuming the best of the best, watch out for those who deserve the worst!

Where do you see yourself in this bloody scene? Are you willing to take up that cross and let some of the blood of Christ rub off on you? Do you lament? Knowing what you know now, do you honor the excruciating pain your Savior suffered? Or do you think that Jesus was crucified on a brass-coated cross between two candles in a colorful, well-lit sanctuary?

Read Hebrews 10:19–39 carefully:

> Therefore, my friends, since we have confidence to enter the sanctuary by the blood of Jesus, by the new and living way that he opened for us through the curtain (that is, through his flesh), and since we have a great priest over the house of God, let us approach with a true heart in full assurance of faith, with our hearts sprinkled clean from an evil conscience and our bodies washed with pure water. Let us hold fast to the confession of our hope without wavering, for he who has promised is faithful. And let us consider how to provoke one another to love and good deeds, not neglecting to meet together as is the habit of some, but encouraging one another, and all the more as you see the day approaching.
>
> For if we willfully persist in sin after having received the knowledge of the truth, there no longer

remains a sacrifice for sins, but a fearful prospect of judgment, and a fury of fire that will consume the adversaries. A man who has violated the law of Moses dies without mercy at the testimony of two or three witnesses. How much worse punishment do you think will be deserved by the man who has spurned the Son of God, and *profaned the blood of the covenant* by which he was sanctified, and outraged the Spirit of grace? For we know him who said, "Vengeance is mine, I will repay." And again, "The Lord will judge his people." It is a fearful thing to fall into the hands of the living God.

But recall the former days when, after you were enlightened, you endured a hard struggle with sufferings, sometimes being publicly exposed to abuse and affliction, and sometimes being partners with those so treated. For you had compassion on the prisoners, and you joyfully accepted the plundering of your property, since you knew that you yourselves had a better possession and an abiding one. Therefore do not throw away your confidence, which has a great reward. For you have need of endurance, so that you may do the will of God and receive what is promised. For yet "in a very little while, the one who is coming will come and will not delay; but my righteous one will live by faith. My soul takes no pleasure in anyone who shrinks back."

But we are not among those who shrink back and so are lost, but among those who have faith and are saved. (Emphasis mine.)

No! We do not "profane the blood of the covenant!" We do not take for granted the agony our Savior suffered for us. We do not sin deliberately knowing that Jesus already died for our sins. We would not be so contemptuous, for we are a part of a new covenant in the blood of Jesus. God, make us all the more a part of your covenant of grace! May we participate in the blood of Christ as true partakers. Far be it from us to glory except in the cross of our Lord, Jesus Christ, by which the world has been crucified to us and we to the world!

A final word from Philippians 2:1–11:

> If then there is any encouragement in Christ, any consolation from love, any sharing in the Spirit, any compassion and sympathy, make my joy complete: be of the same mind, having the same love, being in full accord and of one mind. Do nothing from selfish ambition or conceit, but in humility regard others as better than yourselves. Let each of you look not to your own interests, but to the interests of others. Let the same mind be in you that was in Christ Jesus, who, though he was in the form of God, did not regard equality with God as something to be exploited, but he emptied himself, taking the form of a slave, being born in human likeness. And being found in human form, he humbled himself and became obedient to the point of death—even death on a cross. Therefore God also highly exalted him, and gave him the name that is above every name, so that at the name of Jesus every knee should bend, in heaven and on earth and under the earth, and every tongue should confess that Jesus Christ is Lord to the glory of God the Father.

The Nails

There they crucified him,
and with him two others, one on either side,
with Jesus in between them.
Pilate also had an inscription written and put on the cross. It read,
"Jesus of Nazareth, the King of the Jews."
Many of the Jews read the inscription,
because the place where Jesus was crucified was near the city;
and it was written in Hebrew, in Latin, and in Greek.
Then the chief priests of the Jews said to Pilate,
"Do not write, 'The King of the Jews,' but,
'This man said, I am the King of the Jews.'"
Pilate answered,
"What I have written I have written."
(John 19:18–22)

It can be a very powerful thing to meditate on the Crucifixion of Christ by injecting ourselves into the scene. More often than not, we perceive ourselves as bystanders, helplessly looking on. But we can discover that we as individuals are the crucifiers of Christ. Because He had to suffer for our sins to pay the price of our redemption, we may as well have hammered the nails that held Him to the cross. Just as harsh is the discovery that we might have been in the crowd crying, "Crucify Him!" Or that we may as well have been Pontius Pilate handing Christ over, or the temple guard who bound Him in Gethsemane when He was arrested, or, God forbid, the Pharisees who condemned Him, plotted to have Him arrested, and conspired to get rid of Him. We could have been Peter, who denied Him, or even Judas, who betrayed Him?

More often than not, we can now feel proud to have accepted Christ, accepting His sacrifice for our sins. But how do we perceive our responsibilities for our needs for that sacrifice, that suffering, that punishment that we deserve? Has an innocent person ever taken the responsibility for your mistakes? Christ took the sins you committed on Himself. He took my sins, too. I deserve what He received! You deserve what he endured! What a gracious gift we have received! "While we were still weak, at the right time Christ died for the ungodly! [that's you and me!] Why, one will hardly die for a righteous man—though perhaps for a good man one will dare even to die. But God shows His love for us in that while we were yet sinners Christ died for us. Since, therefore, we are now justified by His blood, much more shall we be saved by Him from the wrath of God" (Romans 5:6–9).

You see, God hates sin. We were created to bring Him glory. But our self-indulgent self-interest brings Him shame. We have dishonored God not only by our lack of respect for His love, for His gracious providence, and for His abundant mercy, but also for His extraordinary grace. He came in the flesh as Jesus Christ. He taught us His way, His truth, and He died for our sins! We live in the age of grace. We are raised in glory by our knowledge of the Resurrection. That passage in Romans 5 goes on: "For if while we were enemies we were reconciled to God by the death of His Son, much more, now that we are reconciled, shall we be saved by His life! Not only so, but we also rejoice in God through our Lord Jesus Christ, through whom we have now received our reconciliation" (vv. 10–11). Reconciliation! Getting back together. God is the one who took the initiative in making up, and God is the one who was offended! Keep listening:

> Therefore, as sin came into the world through one man, and death through sin, and so death spread to all people because all people sinned [sin indeed was in the world before the law was given, but sin is not

counted where there is no law]. Yet death reigned from Adam to Moses, even over those whose sins were not like the transgression of Adam, who was a type of the one who was to come. But the free gift is not like the trespass. For if many died through one man's trespass, much more have the grace of God, and the free gift, in the grace of that one man Jesus Christ abounded for many! And the free gift is not like the effect of that one man's sin. For the judgment following one trespass brought condemnation, but the free gift following many trespasses brings justification. (Romans 5:12–16)

Justification, being set right. God is the one who sets us right. We can't do it for ourselves. Again, God took the initiative! "If, because of one man's trespass, death reigned through that one man, much more will those who receive the abundance of grace and the free gift of righteousness reign in life through the one man Jesus Christ. Therefore, just as one man's trespass led to condemnation for all people, so one man's act of righteousness leads to acquittal and life for all men. For just as by one man's disobedience many were made sinners, so by one man's obedience many will be made righteous" (vv. 10–19).

One man's act of righteousness, and one man's obedience! We are the benefactors of Christ's sacrificial act on the cross. The cross. The Crucifixion. In an article from the *Journal of The American Medical Association*, published in 1986 and entitled, "On the Physical Death of Jesus Christ," a pathologist (Gary L. Fanning, MD) and a pastor worked together to describe the medical aspects of the torture of the Crucifixion:

Having condemned Christ to death, Pilate ordered Him to be "scourged" and crucified. The practice of scourging, by law, preceded every Roman execution. The condemned man (women, senators, and soldiers were exempt) was tied to a post after being stripped and was beaten with a small whip made of several thongs, into the ends of which were woven small metal balls and shards of bone. The severity of the beating often determined how long the victim would live on the cross. In addition to horrible pain, scourging produced blood loss that frequently caused shock, leaving the victim just short of death. Following the beating, the victim was mocked and taunted and, accompanied by a Roman guard, made to carry the crossbar of his cross to the site of crucifixion. Because Christ was unable to carry his own crossbar, it is highly probable that His scourging was especially brutal.

The practice of crucifixion was initially carried out on a tree or upright post. The Romans learned this practice from the Carthaginians and perfected it as a means of slow, maximally painful torture and death. Having carried the crossbar to the site of crucifixion, the victim was stripped of his clothing, thrown to the ground on his back (newly and badly wounded already from the scourging), and his arms were fixed to the crossbar by nails driven through the wrists. The victim and crossbar were then lifted by four soldiers, and the crossbar was attached to the upright post. The victim's feet were next attached to the cross by bending the legs and nailing the feet to the front of the post.

Once crucified, the victim might live for hours or days, depending on his general condition, the severity of the scourging, and the disposition of the Roman soldiers. Death usually resulted from a combination of factors. Blood loss from the scourging often left the victim near death, as was the case with Jesus. Crucifixion greatly upsets the balance of breathing, making it almost impossible to exhale without great effort and unbearable pain. The mixture of shock and suffocation leads to fatal rhythms of the heart, most notably, ventricular fibrillation, which is probably what led to the death of Jesus and would explain the suddenness of this death on the cross. The soldiers would frequently break the victim's legs to hasten death and would almost routinely insert a spear into the right side of the chest aimed at the heart to guarantee that death had occurred before the victim was removed from the cross. If the family did not receive permission to have the body removed from the cross immediately after death, it might be left on the cross for days to be attacked by predatory animals and birds. Joseph of Arimathea obtained permission from Pilate to have Christ's body removed for entombment, but Pilate, amazed at the suddenness of Christ's demise, would not give permission until a centurion confirmed that death had occurred.

Think, for a moment, just of the puncture wounds caused by those nails. It makes me wince to think of the hammer pounding the nails through Christ's wrists. If His arms had been strapped to the crossbeam, nails in the hands would have been adequate if only to prevent Him from slipping out of the bindings. And even if He had been able to do so, falling from the cross, His feet would have become so badly wounded, perhaps His ankles would have been so badly twisted that He would never have been able to walk again. But because of the gravity of being suspended in an upright position, with His hands higher than His heart, His hands would have stopped bleeding right away. However, blood would have continued to drip from the wounds in His feet.

The nails in His feet supported His weight. The difficulty with exhaling in such a position would have made Him try to lift Himself up just enough to let out air. Speaking in sentences would have been nearly impossible. Imagine putting your whole weight on the nails (or possibly, a single nail) in your feet. It is not too likely that His cross had a platform to which His feet were nailed. They would have been nailed directly to the post, held in place by two men as another hammered the nail.

Our Savior received this torture because of our sins. He suffered for the sins of the world and for the sins to come—yours and mine— and for every sin committed for almost two thousand years now. That's a lot of sin. It was a lot of suffering. We are the guilty ones. He was innocent. We are imperfect, fallen human flesh. He is the perfect, divine incarnation of God. Only God taking that torture could make the difference for all time. And ever since that Friday so long ago, the world has been able to know the fullness of God's grace. Do you know it? Is it not amazing? Yes. It is!

Let us do our best to never hurt Him again. Perhaps if we could feel those nails just a little bit, we would really want to change. Think about the pain Jesus suffered for your sins. Can you feel it? If not, give thanks!

A Prayer

Oh, almighty God, Lord, Jesus Christ: We do not know how many blows of the hammer it took to nail you to the cross. We can't imagine how much you actually suffered on our behalf, but we know you felt forsaken. Help us to appreciate the fact that you died substituting for us, taking our place on the cross, dying for our sins. Help us to repay your gracious act of redemption with true repentance and a sincere effort of letting your Holy Spirit live in us. For we are crucified with Christ. It is no longer we who live, but Christ who lives in us. So be it! Amen.

The Spear

When the soldiers had crucified Jesus,
they took his clothes and divided them into
four parts, one for each soldier.
They also took his tunic;
now the tunic was seamless, woven in one piece from the top.
So they said to one another, "Let us not tear it,
but cast lots for it to see who will get it."
This was to fulfill what the scripture says,
"They divided my clothes among themselves,
and for my clothing they cast lots."
And that is what the soldiers did.
Meanwhile, standing near the cross of Jesus were his mother,
and his mother's sister, Mary, the wife of
Clopas, and Mary Magdalene.
When Jesus saw his mother
and the disciple whom he loved standing beside her,
he said to his mother, "Woman, here is your son."
Then he said to the disciple,
"Here is your mother."
And from that hour the disciple took her into his own home.
After this, when Jesus knew that all was now finished,
he said (in order to fulfill the scriptures),
"I am thirsty."
A jar full of sour wine was standing there.
So they put a sponge full of the wine on a branch of hyssop a

nd held it to his mouth. When he had received the wine, he said,
"It is finished."
Then he breathed his last and gave up his spirit.
Since it was the day of Preparation,
the Jews did not want the bodies left on
the cross during the sabbath,
especially because that sabbath was a day of great solemnity.
So they asked Pilate to have the legs of the crucified men broken
and the bodies removed.
Then the soldiers came and broke the legs
of the first and of the other
who had been crucified with him.
But when they came to Jesus
and saw that he was already dead,
they did not break his legs.
Instead one of the soldiers pierced his side
with a spear,
and at once blood and water came out.
These things occurred so that the scripture might be fulfilled,
"None of his bones shall be broken."
And again another passage of scripture says,
"They will look on the one whom they have pierced."
(John 19:23–37)

Jeremiah spoke in an oracle about the coming day of the Lord:

> Thus says the Lord, who stretched out the heavens
> and founded the earth and formed the spirit of man
> within him: 'Lo, I am about to make Jerusalem a
> cup of reeling to all the peoples round about ... On
> that Day, I will make Jerusalem a heavy stone for
> all the peoples; all who lift it shall grievously hurt
> themselves. On that Day, I will make the clans of
> Judah ... like a flaming torch among sheaves. ...
> On that Day, the Lord will put a shield about the

inhabitants of Jerusalem so that the feeblest among them on that Day shall be like David, and the house of David shall be like God, like the angel of the Lord, at their head … And I will pour out on the house of David and the inhabitants of Jerusalem a spirit of compassion and supplication, so that, when they look on Him whom they have pierced, they shall mourn for Him as one mourns for an only child, and weep bitterly over Him as one weeps over a firstborn.'" (Zechariah 12:1–10)

Look at Him. The one who has been pierced is Jesus! God pours upon us a spirit of compassion and prayer as we fix our eyes on the crucified body of our Lord. Look at Him. What do you see?

Do you see a defeated dreamer or a sacrificial Lamb? Do you see the end of a life or a finished work? What was finished? In the death of Christ, we are able to see the birth of forgiveness! In the death of Christ, we are able to see the death of sin! In the death of Christ, we are able to see God "making peace by the blood of His cross" (Colossians 1:20).

Isaiah proclaimed:

Yet it was the will of the Lord to bruise Him; He has put Him to grief; when He makes Himself an offering for sin, He shall see His offspring, He shall prolong His days; the will of the Lord shall prosper in His hand; He shall see the fruit of the travail of His soul and be satisfied. By His knowledge shall the righteous One, my Servant, make many to be accounted righteous; and He shall bear their iniquities. Therefore, I will divide Him a portion among the great, and He shall divide the spoil with the strong; because He poured out His soul to death, and was numbered with the transgressors; yet He bore the sin

of many, and made intercession for the transgressors!
(Isaiah 53:10–12)

Look at Him, whose suffering was total, and realize that, as
He poured out His soul, He was filling your cup. As He bore our
iniquities, He gained more than just a portion of glory. He became
the greatest of the great, the King of kings and Lord of lords. Look
at Him. As He offered Himself, He envisioned you, the church,
the offspring of His gracious atonement and the fruit of His travail.
His days have been prolonged as the day of the Lord echoed down
through the centuries, and the will of God prospered in *His* hand as
we continue to do it. Look at Him!

Look at whose side they pierced. Only in John is the piercing
of Christ's side mentioned. In John, Jesus spoke his final words,
"It is finished," and then, it seems, he quietly bowed His head and
gave up His Spirit (19:30). In the gospel of John, you almost get the
impression that His dying moment was hardly noticed.

Normally, the Romans left the victims on their crosses long after
their deaths. If life lingered, the Romans would leave them hanging
day after day in the heat of the sun and the cold of the night, tortured
by thirst and gnats and flies that crawled especially in and out of
the welts of their wounds. Often, these victims died in the raving
madness that ensued.

On that Friday, so long ago, as the day was drawing to an end,
the Jewish leaders expressed concern about the approaching Sabbath
festival of the Passover. They wanted things to be tidied up a bit,
and three crucified, dying, or dead bodies wouldn't be proper. What
hypocrites they are made out to be as John paints a portrayal of the
farce of their faith. The soldiers began to finish their job with the
gross and cruel method of taking their hammers and breaking the
legs of the crucified men in order to, in a way, detonate their systems
with such a blast that the blow brought death. But when they came
to Jesus, they finally noticed that he was already dead!

In Matthew, Mark, and Luke, as the story is told, there is no
doubt as to the exact moment of Jesus's death. It happened at "about

the ninth hour" (Matthew 27:46, 15:34; Luke 23:44), or 3:00 p.m. The sky had been dark since noon. Then, "Jesus cried out again with a loud voice and yielded up His Spirit" (Matthew 27:50; Mark 15:37). Just before He dies, Luke reports Jesus as saying, "Father, into your hands I commend my Spirit" (23:46). In all three, Jesus's moment of death was a very noticeable event. From Matthew: "And behold, the curtain of the Temple was torn in two, from top to bottom; and the earth shook, and the rocks split; the tombs also were opened, and many bodies of the saints who had fallen asleep were raised ... When the centurion and those who were with him keeping watch over Jesus saw the earthquake and what took place, they were filled with awe, and said, 'Truly this man was the Son of God'" (Mark 15:38–39; Matthew 27:51–54). In Luke, he says, "Certainly this man was innocent" (23:47).

In John, however, the moment of Jesus's death was missed by the soldiers. But now, as the day is drawing to its end, they must finish their day's task and dispose of the bodies. Jesus's legs did not need to be broken, but to ensure His death, one of them pierced His side with a spear. And in that moment, from that final wound, there flowed blood and water. Communion and baptism: the covenant of forgiveness and the covenant of cleansing grace and new life. I can't say it better than when we sing: "Rock of ages, cleft for me, let me hide myself in Thee. Let the water and the blood, from Thy wounded side which flowed, be of sin the double cure: save from death, and make me pure" ("Toplady," 1763).

Although it cannot be confirmed, scholars speculate that the spear pierced Jesus's heart, and the blood left in His heart when it stopped pumping became mingled with the fluid of the pericardium and came forth as the spear was pulled back, tearing apart the heart of our Savior. I'm not sure how long it takes, but another thought is that, in the course of the time between His death and the piercing of His side, the blood in Jesus's heart began to separate into red blood cells and white blood cells. The white cells would have appeared as an almost-clear liquid as it came from the wound in His side. Even so, what little blood was left in His body was completely drained. Jesus was dead.

Look at Him. Look at whose side they pierced. Jesus was dead. His body had no life. The one who, by His nature, was truly God and truly human was no longer alive in the physical form. The flesh-and-blood human nature of our Savior, Jesus, was dead. But the Holy Word, the omnipotent God, the divine nature of Christ—well, that's another story!

A Prayer

Almighty God, Lord Christ, we are faced with the horrible reality that in Jesus, you truly died. It leaves us reeling. We, too, must die someday. But in death, Jesus has led the way. Because He goes before us, let us trust that as we follow Him, our deaths will not be as heartbreaking as we might imagine, should we not have faith in His amazing grace. For we know that He is the lamb of God who takes away the sins of the world! For this, we give great thanks. In Jesus's honor and with grateful hearts we pray, amen.

The Tomb

After these things, Joseph of Arimathea,
who was a disciple of Jesus,
though a secret one because of his fear of the Jews,
asked Pilate to let him take away the body of Jesus.
Pilate gave him permission; so he came and removed his body.
Nicodemus, who had at first come to Jesus by night,
also came, bringing a mixture of myrrh and aloes,
weighing about a hundred pounds.
They took the body of Jesus and wrapped it with the spices
in linen cloths, according to the burial custom of the Jews.
Now there was a garden in the place where he was crucified,
and in the garden there was a new tomb
in which no one had ever been laid.
And so, because it was the day of Preparation,
and the tomb was nearby,
they laid Jesus there.
(John 19:38–42)

The body of Jesus was buried. The Jewish custom included the use of a mixture of myrrh and aloes, not for embalming, but to stifle the scent of death a bit. The use of about a hundred pounds of myrrh and aloes is remarkable because this is the amount that would be used for the burial of a very wealthy man. Using linen cloths to wrap the body was also an extravagant expense and would not have been used for criminals. The gospel of Mark tells us that Joseph of Arimathea bought the shroud for Jesus's burial that day. Some scholars speculate that because the gospel of Matthew tells us that the tomb was Joseph of Arimathea's own new tomb, he was expecting to die fairly soon and had spared no expense in his preparations. But it all went to Jesus instead. The tomb, which was in a garden area, would have been in the backyard of a very wealthy family.

What little is revealed about Joseph of Arimathea seems to indicate that he had been deeply touched by Christ somehow. He was a Jewish leader who, for fear of the Jews, felt he could only be a disciple secretly until that point. The risk seemed over with Jesus's death, and he exposed his faith—and so does Nicodemus, as they arrange for the burial of Jesus's body. The gospel of John says nothing of the need to guard the tomb, let alone to set a seal upon it. That story is only in Matthew!

Although there is the impression of haste, John does say that the Jews' burial custom was followed. We presume that things must have fallen into place fairly quickly, because the burial had to happen before the setting of the sun, and the Day of Passover had begun, which would have lasted from Friday evening to sunset on Saturday. Because of this, we imagine the closing of the tomb occurring as the sun went down, and Joseph and Nicodemus returned to their homes unclean in the darkness of the Sabbath's rest, and therefore unable to go to the Temple in the morning because they touched a dead body.

The Savior they believed in had been buried. There in the tomb lay the source of their hopes and the inspiration of their faith. There lay the silenced voice of compassion and the wisdom of the truth. There lay the one who could heal by His touch and love with His words. All that Jesus meant, in some respects, was buried with Him. That's why the graves of the ones we love seem to be an important place to visit. There, our memories unfold, and the meanings of their lives return to us. And even though we know that meaning is not in this spot where their earthly remains exist, burial sites can still be an important place of remembrance.

Darcie Sims, a grief counselor and an author who lost a young child to the cruel disease of cancer, tells a story about a weekend workshop held for members of an organization called Compassionate

Friends. The workshop was particularly for those whose children had been killed violently by murder or by drunken drivers. On attendees' nametags were also the names and ages of the children who had died.

One woman had been deeply touched by one of Darcie's talks and spoke to her personally about her grief during some free time. The woman was in her late forties, and her daughter had been six when she died. It had obviously been a long time ago, but the woman's grief still seemed fresh. Darcie said, "Tell me about your daughter," and the woman spoke about the murder—when it happened, where it happened, how her daughter had been found, and all about the beautiful funeral that had been held. After many minutes, Darcie again said, "Tell me about your *daughter*," and the woman spoke about the murderer, the trial, the jury, and the conviction. She shared what she knew about the prison the murderer was in and a little about his daily routine. After several more minutes of listening, Darcie said, "Tell me. What color were your daughter's eyes?" The woman fell apart, buried her head in Darcie's shoulder, and sobbed. "I can't remember," she said.

After they cried together for several minutes, Darcie asked if the woman had a picture. Picking through her purse, she found her wallet. Slowly, she opened it up and found a picture. Taking it out of the blurry old plastic cover, her tears began to flow again as they saw the little girl's face. Finally, the woman said, "They were blue."

There will be encouraging reminders to us of the meaning of the life that's been lost, and there will be reminders that perpetuate our grief. All the morbid remembrances of Jesus's bloody death give meaning to our lives only insofar as we keep the realization before us that His death is our death. His suffering is our suffering. And as we face His tomb in silence, we remember not only Jesus who was buried there, but also that, on the third day, by God's awesome and mysterious power, He was resurrected as Christ, overcoming death, conquering the grave, and opening the glory of eternal life to us. His Resurrection is our resurrection!

Was there blood in the tomb? Were there soaked-through linen cloths? Had they cleaned Jesus up a bit? The Shroud of Turin was supposedly the shroud in which Jesus was buried. (I can accept that.) Did it have some blood stains on it? Joseph of Arimathea had handled the body of Jesus. Did he get some of Jesus's blood on his hands? What does that mean to you? What does the blood of Christ, the things that caused Him to bleed, and the things that were touched by His blood all mean to you?

Your Son's Love

A story, written in the year 2000 for an Easter sunrise service. How sad that, in so many ways, it all came true twenty years later.

The day is over. You are driving home. You tune in your radio. You hear a little blurb about a village in India where some villagers have died suddenly, strangely, of a flu that has never been seen before. It's not influenza, but three or four people are dead, and its reality is of interest, so they're sending some doctors over there to investigate. You don't think much about it, but on Sunday, coming home from church, you hear another radio spot about it. Only this time, they say it's not three villagers; it's thirty thousand villagers in the back hills of this particular area, and it will be on TV that night. CNN runs a blurb; people are heading there from the disease control center in Atlanta because this disease strain has never been seen before.

By Monday morning when you get up, it's the lead story in the news. Now, it's not just India; it's Pakistan, Afghanistan, Iran, and, before you know it, you're hearing this story everywhere, and they have coined it as "the mystery flu." The president has commented that he and everyone are praying and hoping that all will go well ...over there. But everyone is wondering, "How are we going to contain it?" That's when the president of France makes an announcement that shocks Europe. He is closing their borders. No flights from India, Pakistan, or any of the countries where this disease has been seen may enter the country. That's why that night, you are watching a little bit of CNN before going to bed. Your jaw hits your chest when a weeping woman is translated from a French news program into English: There's a man lying in a hospital in Paris dying of the mystery flu. It has come to Europe.

Panic strikes. The best they can tell is that, once you get it, you have it for a week before you know about it. Then you have four days of unbelievable symptoms, and then you die. Britain closes its doors, but it's too late. South Hampton, Liverpool, North Hampton are affected. It's Tuesday morning when the president of the United States makes the following announcement: "Due to a national security risk, all flights to and from Europe and Asia have been canceled. If your loved ones are overseas, I'm sorry. They cannot come back until we find a cure for this thing."

Within four days the United States has been plunged into an unbelievable fear. People are selling little masks for your face. People are talking about, "What if it comes to this country?" Preachers on Tuesday are saying, "It's the scourge of God." It's Wednesday night, and you are at a church prayer meeting when somebody runs in from the parking lot and says, "Turn on a radio! Turn on a radio!" And while the church listens to a little transistor radio with a microphone stuck up to it, the announcement is made: "Two women are lying in a Long Island hospital, dying from the mystery flu!"

Within hours, it seems, this thing just sweeps across the country. People are working around the clock, trying to find an antidote. Nothing is working. California, Oregon, Arizona, Florida, and Massachusetts are all reporting new cases. It's as though it's just sweeping in from the borders. And then, just as suddenly, the news comes out: The code has been broken. A cure can be found, and a vaccine can be made. It's going to take the blood of somebody who hasn't been infected by infectious illnesses, and sure enough, all through the Midwest, through all those channels of emergency broadcasting, everyone is asked to do one simple thing: go to your downtown hospital or local clinic and have your blood type taken. That's all they ask of you. When you hear the sirens go off in your neighborhood, you are asked to please make your way quickly, quietly, and safely to the local hospitals and clinics.

Sure enough, when you and your family get down there late on that Friday night, there is a long line, and they've got nurses and doctors coming out to prick fingers and take blood and put labels on little test tubes. Your spouse and your kids are out there, and they take your blood type, and say, "Wait here in the parking lot, and if we call your name, you can be dismissed and go home."

You stand around, apprehensive, with your neighborhood, wondering what is going on and if this is the end of the world. Suddenly, a young man in a white lab coat comes running out of the hospital, screaming. He's yelling a name and waving a clipboard. What? He yells it again. Your son tugs on your jacket and says, "Daddy, that's me." Before you know it, they have grabbed your boy. Wait a minute! Hold on! They say, "It's okay, his blood is clean. His blood is pure. We want to make sure he doesn't have the disease. We think he's got the right type." Five tense minutes later, out come the doctors and nurses, crying and hugging one another. Some are even laughing with relief. It's the first time you have seen anyone laugh in a week, and an older doctor walks up to you and says, "Thank you, sir. Your son's blood type is perfect. It's clean, it is pure, and we can make a vaccine."

As the word begins to spread all across the parking lot, people are screaming and praying and laughing and crying. But then the gray-haired doctor pulls you and your wife aside and says, "May I see you for a moment? We didn't realize that the donor would be a young boy, and we need … we need you to sign a consent form."

You begin to sign, and then you see that the number of pints of blood to be taken is empty. "How many pints?" you ask.

And that is when the old doctor's smile fades and he says, "We had no idea it would be a little child. We weren't prepared. We need it all!"

"B–but, but … I don't understand," you say.

"We are talking about the world here. Please sign. We need it all," the doctor says.

"But can't you give him a transfusion?"

"If we had clean blood, we would. Can you sign? Would you sign?"

In numb silence, you do. Then they say, "Would you like to have a moment with him before we begin?"

Could you walk back to the room where your son sits on a table, saying, "Daddy? What's going on?"

Can you take his hands and say, "Son, you know I love you, and I would never ever let anything happen to you that didn't just have to be, right? Do you understand that?"

And when the doctor comes back and says, "I'm sorry, we've got to get started. People all over the world are dying," could you leave?

Could you walk out while your son is saying, "Dad! Dad! Why have you forsaken me?"

And then, next week, when they have the ceremony to honor your son and some folks sleep through it, and some folks don't even come because they go to the lake, and some folks come with pretentious smiles and just pretend to care, would you want to jump up and say, "My son died for you! Don't you care?"

Is that what God wants to say? "My son died for you! Don't you know how much I care?" Consider the gift of Christ's sacrifice for our sins from God, the Father's point of view touches our hearts in a special way. Just think about the love God has given us!

PART V

The Seven Last Words

It seems appropriate to conclude a book of meditations on the Passion of Christ with a serious look at "the seven last words of Christ," spoken from the cross. It has been a Good Friday worship experience several times in my career, where different pastors from the community would each share a meditation on one of the things Jesus said as He was dying.

Jesus mustered the strength to speak even as He suffered so severely. He expressed forgiveness, He showed concern for His mother, He expressed forsakenness and thirst, and Jesus claimed a completion of His purpose. And finally, at the moment of His death, He committed His Spirit into the hands of His Father, God. He knew He would suffer. He didn't want to as a human, but He surrendered His life to the will of God. It is difficult to absorb all that happened, but we all need to realize that He did it in our place.

The last section of my gallery on the Passion of Christ is in the back. You see everything else before you get there. I just hope you have kept in mind the final triumph we will all know because of the Resurrection.

There is an important verse we need to keep in mind: "We rejoice in our suffering" (Romans 5:3, ESV).

Father, Forgive Them

Two others also, who were criminals, were led
away to be put to death with him. When they
came to the place that is called the skull,
they crucified Jesus there with the criminals,
one on his right and one on his left.
Then Jesus said,
"Father, forgive them; for they do not know what they are doing."
(Luke 23:32–34a)

One day, a great king dressed himself as a commoner and went out among his subjects to see how they perceived life in the kingdom he ruled. At a tavern at one end of the town, he broke up a brawl and insisted the fighting men shake hands and part as friends. He told them that they should direct themselves to the fighting of the enemies of their king, not one another. One man responded by telling him that the king should go and fight his own battles. And he thought, *If only they knew the battles I fight for them every day, trying to rule fairly for all.*

In another area, he noticed barefoot children in ragged clothes. He sought out their mother, a widow, and asked why the children had no shoes and why they were so poorly clothed. She told him that her landlord took all the money she had left so she could stay in her home. But he asked, "Isn't the king your landlord?"

She said, "Yes, and the man he sends to take our rent and taxes is always asking for more." And she said that because of that, she hated the king. Then he gave her a bag full of enough money for a year's worth of taxes. She was grateful to him. And he thought, *If only she knew that I was the king, perhaps she would stop hating me.*

Then he sought out the tax collector who had taken so much from the poor widow. When he found him, he began to ask questions. Thinking he might be a spy from the royal court, the tax collector had his henchmen beat the king and leave him for dead. And in his pain, he thought, *If only they knew that I was their king and had shown them much favor, they would not have treated me so poorly. They would be fair, as I have ordered them to be fair.*

As he lay dying, a man who was his enemy came by. Not knowing he was the king, but having compassion for him because he was wounded, he helped him and nursed him back to health. And the king thought, *This man does not know that I am the king, but we are no longer enemies.*

When the king returned to his palace, he told the story of where he'd been and what had happened, but the members of his court rebuked him for doing such a risky thing. And they said among themselves, "If only we had known he'd become a commoner, we could have taken over his throne."

If only they knew. If only they knew. If only they knew that Jesus was really the Messiah, would they still have crucified him? But there he was, dying. And rather than think of his own suffering, he prayed for others. There he was, dying for their sins, for your sins and for my sins—for the sins of the whole world—and Jesus was claiming his purpose while he fulfilled it: "Father, forgive them" (Luke 23:3). Even though they were his executioners, Jesus still died for their sins. Even though they reject him, Jesus sacrificed himself for their sake.

They didn't know what they were doing. What is it that they didn't know? Perhaps they didn't know how painful it was to be crucified. Perhaps they didn't know that He loved them so much that He would die to save their souls. Perhaps they didn't know the truth He could teach; they didn't know His healing power; they didn't know His holy purpose; they didn't know His heavenly grace. Because if they did, they would not condemn Him; they would love

Him. Perhaps they didn't know that this was the incarnation of God that they were putting to death.

They didn't know what they were doing. What was it they were doing that they didn't understand? Perhaps they didn't understand that they were condemning an innocent man. Perhaps they didn't understand they were betraying the Lord. Perhaps they didn't understand that they were denying the truth. Perhaps they didn't understand that they were taking the most wonderful gift they'd been given and throwing it all away. And perhaps they didn't understand that they were fulfilling God's purpose by bringing death to God's Son, and thereby fulfilling the plan of divine redemption.

Who did Jesus forgive here? He forgave the Roman soldiers who didn't know what they were doing because they didn't know the blessing of faith, the promise of the Hebrew scriptures, or the hope of the kingdom of heaven. He forgave those who taunted Him and mocked Him and treated Him like the worst sort of criminal, when, in fact, He was God. He forgave the Jews who brought about this wicked travesty of justice out of the fear of their social and moral prominence to Jesus. He forgave them! He forgave the passersby and the unknowing onlookers who seemed so indifferent, so uninterested that they didn't even bother to find out who He was, and they didn't even care if it hurt to have nails through His hands and feet. Jesus Christ forgave His crucifiers. And that's also you and me every time we sin. Because He blots out that sin by His death. We deserve that punishment, but He received it! He died in our places! He suffered so we could go free!

And he said, "Father, forgive them, for they do not know what they are doing." They didn't know that what they were doing while His death meant receiving their freedom from sin, receiving forgiveness, and receiving another chance!

If only they knew. If only they knew. *Tell them!* Children, your sins are forgiven! Father, forgive them, for they do not know what they are doing.

It's not as if it's okay to do evil or to sin if you don't know any better. Ignorance is no license to relinquish moral responsibility. We can't pretend to live in the dark because we can sympathize. We can feel the pain of someone hurting; we can feel the anguish of someone suffering and of someone who is persecuted. We can know better because we can put ourselves in his or her place, and we can know right from wrong because of that. We can know what is good for others by knowing what is good for us. And by knowing what is good for us, we can treat others as we would have others treat us. We can know better. We should always let this idea be our guiding principle. It's the principle by which Jesus lived. Such moral reasoning doesn't take a great faith. But it's there by the grace of God, and it is like a seed. If we help it grow, faith will come. And faith will help us understand.

Father, forgive us, especially when we choose not knowing or not understanding.

A Prayer

Almighty God, You gave Your Son Jesus to be our redeemer. He sets us free from sin by His suffering in our place. We are grateful for all He's done for us. Help us to live as forgiven people, as people who know the truth. We know what we are doing by following Christ's example of sacrifice. Give us grace to learn it well. This we pray in Jesus' name. Amen.

Behold, Your Son

Meanwhile, standing near the cross of Jesus
were his mother, and his mother's sister, Mary, the wife of Clopas,
and Mary Magdalene.
When Jesus saw his mother and the disciple whom he
loved standing beside her, he said to his mother,
"Woman, behold your son."
Then he said to his disciple,
"Here is your mother."
And from that hour the disciple took her into his own home.
(John 19:26–27)

In the 1300s, there was a dyer in the Italian town of Siena, who had a daughter named Catherine. She had a wonderful faith, and even as a little girl, when she would pray, it always seemed as if she were talking directly to God. At times, she would even fill in God's part of the conversation with words that could only have been placed in her heart by God.

She became a Dominican nun in Siena, and, a bit of a mystic, her writings were concerned about the constant yearning of the soul for oneness with God. Her most famous work is, naturally, *The Dialogues of St. Catherine of Siena*. In it there is a beautiful section that speaks of how there seems to be five kinds of tears that correspond with the various states of the soul. it is written as a dialogue between the soul and truth, and it begins with the longing of the soul to learn from the truth about how these tears came to be and about the result of the heart's weeping.

The five kinds of tears are:

1. Tears of death, caused by sin.
2. Tears of fear, caused by guilt. Here, she notes that "the eye weeps in order to satisfy the grief of the heart."
3. Tears of sorrow mingled with joy. Sorrow for grief, caused by sin, and joy for the hope of mercy as the goodness of the truth begins to become known.
4. Tears of love: love of truth and love of neighbor. These tears are not for self, but for others.
5. Tears of peace as the heart unites with truth in love and finds its rest in the eternal presence of God. These are, again, a mixture of tears of joy and sorrow as one begins to weep with those who weep and rejoice with those who rejoice.

But these then give way to tears of fire, which, though invisible, are the tears of one who desires to weep but cannot. They are shed because the heart feels the love of God so strongly that the soul then cries about feeling the same love for others with which it knows it is loved.

Catherine of Siena rose to a position of leadership and was able to have some influence in having the papacy moved from Avignon in France back to Rome. And in 1461, she was canonized as a saint. But her words about love and tears seem very relevant today, especially in reflecting on the tears of fire—the tears of one who desires to weep but cannot. These are tears of love for someone, felt in the knowledge of God's great love for them. Tears are not mentioned in the narrative of the Crucifixion of Christ, but tears just as true, well up behind the words, "Woman, behold your son ..." (John 19:26).

I believe that, for every woman, it is possible to look upon her children at any age and remember them as infants. And I'm sure it's not too difficult to remember, not only their births, but the beginnings of the children's lives within their mothers. For nine months or so, each child is, in effect, one with its mother. The life of the one depends on the life of the other. The life of the infant within the womb depends on the life of the mother who bears the child.

Consider for a moment how the life of Jesus, God made flesh, depended, for a while, on Mary, the mother of Christ. In that oneness, Mary was one with God. Mary became the bridge across which God walked into the world. "How shall this be," Mary said, "since I have no husband?" And the angel said to her, "The Holy Spirit will come upon you, and the power of the most high will overshadow you; therefore the child to be born will be called holy, the son of God" (Luke 1:34–35). And if Mary was still unable to understand, the angel finally told her that "with God, nothing will be impossible" (Luke 1:37). And Mary said, "Behold, I am the handmaid of the Lord." "Behold your son."

Mary's was a life of surrender. She surrendered to the power of God as it entered into her life in a way more real than any of us can imagine. She was no longer her own, but Christ's. And we, likewise, are called upon and challenged not to do our own wills, but God's. "You are not your own," Paul said. "You were bought with a price" (1 Corinthians 6:19–20). What is the price of the tears of fire?

Mary never could have forgotten the oneness she had experienced. I have never been able to appreciate the dramatized stories of Christ's life where they depict His mother as not understanding what Jesus was doing or as unaware that he was the Messiah! He is the Son of God, and Mary is His mother. Mary had been overshadowed by the power of the Holy Spirit! She knew. She had carried God within her. She had been filled with the very presence of the Holy Spirit. Her surrender was for God's glory. And in that surrender, there were tears.

There were tears of joy at the conception of life, tears of pain and happiness at the moment of birth. And now, there were tears at the moment of that child's death. These tears perhaps were not shed but were felt just the same. These tears were not unlike those her son had shed beside the tomb of Lazarus (John 11:35). Tears of grief were mingled with the joy of hope in the knowledge that his friend would soon have life again because Jesus is the Resurrection and the life. Jesus wept. My friends, ours is a God who cried.

And then there were the tears at Gethsemane where he told Peter and James and John, "My soul is very sorrowful, even to death" (Mark 14:34). They were sorrowful because of life, not fear. They were sorrowful because His life was at its end, and He was to leave behind all those He loved. He was sorrowful unto death because His death would hurt the ones He loved. The very soul of God was aching for the souls of all God's other children the way Mary's, at the cross, felt as she beheld her son.

On the way to Calvary, there were tears. On the road that led Him to His place of execution, they seized Simon of Cyrene and made him carry the cross. Following that devastating scene, there was a great multitude of people and of women who bewailed and lamented Him. And Jesus turned to them and said, "Daughters of Jerusalem, do not weep for me, but weep for yourselves and for your children. For behold the days are coming when they will say, 'Blessed are the barren, and the wombs that never bore, and the breasts that never nursed'" (Luke 23:26–29). I wonder if His mother heard those words! I wonder if she heard His words blessing those who could never know the grief of losing a child the way she was losing hers. "Do not weep for me," He said. "Do not weep for me, but weep for yourselves."

What do you have to lose? What would you be leaving behind if the time comes when "they will begin to say to the mountains, 'Fall on us,' and to the hills, 'Cover us!' For if they do this when the wood is green, what will happen when it is dry?" (Luke 23:28–31). If they crucified Christ when the truth was obvious, what will happen if it is obscured? If they did this when faith was claimed, what will happen when doubt runs rampant? If they did this when our eyes were weeping, what will happen when our tears run dry? What will happen when we want to cry but cannot?

Woman, behold your son (John 19:26). Look at what they've done. Look at where this life has led. Does Mary remember Simeon, who was promised by God that he would not die before he saw the Messiah, who came into the temple when Joseph and Mary brought Jesus there to dedicate Him to God eight days after His birth, and took Him in his arms, perhaps even with tears of joy in his eyes, praising God and proclaiming salvation, and then saying to Mary, "Behold, this child is set for the fall and rising of many in Israel, and for a sign that is spoken against (and a sword will pierce through your own soul also)" (Luke 2:34–35). Behold. Behold your son.

Your son was dying for the sins of the world, Mary. Your son was dying. And some of the last words she heard Him say were out of concern for her. She had been the mother of a heavenly child, and now, he appointed her to be the mother of an earthly child.

If, in His day, a widow with no children had nowhere to belong, Jesus provided for her with these words from the cross. These were His last words of hope until His very end, when He committed His spirit to the trust of God.

"When Jesus saw His mother and the disciple whom He loved standing near, He said to His mother, 'Woman, behold, your son.' Then He said to the disciple, 'Behold your mother!' And from that hour the disciple took her to his own home" (John 19:26–27). A place to belong for the mother of heaven, a place on earth.

I wonder, where do you feel you belong? Does it bring you tears of joy? Who else makes your heart begin to weep? Who else can we cry for? Who needs our tears?

A Prayer

Almighty God, Your Son has gone to Your house in order to prepare a place for us. Help us see the promise of belonging in His gracious vision. Our belonging to You is a gift He has given. May we cherish the hope this gives us and may we reflect it like a great light that shines for the whole world. This we pray in Jesus' name. Amen.

Today, You Will Be
with Me in Paradise

One of the criminals who were hanged there
kept deriding him and saying,
"Are you not the Messiah? Save yourself and us."
But the other rebuked him, saying,
"Do you not fear God,
since you are under the same sentence of condemnation?
And we indeed have been condemned justly,
for we are getting what we deserve for our deeds,
but this man has done nothing wrong."
Then he said,
"Jesus, remember me when you come into your kingdom."
He replied,
"Truly I tell you, today you will be with me in paradise."
(Luke 23:39–43)

Is heaven so easy to achieve, is it so simple a thing, is it so free that someone so obviously unfaithful as to be condemned as a criminal and sentenced to death can be worthy of its blessing? Is Jesus so accepting, so merciful, so kind as to welcome into His kingdom a person who is not only a stranger but is a corrupt, distorted, and evil sinner?

Yes. The answer is yes! Heaven is easy! It is simple. It is free. Jesus is that accepting. He is that merciful. He is that kind, ...if we repent. If only we believe. If we accept Him for who He is. Jesus *is* a special gift being given by God, and it is our part to receive that gift, to accept Him, and to let Him into our hearts.

The two everlasting kinds of person hang on either side of Jesus. One man, made bitter by the pain of life, is angry because of his guilt. He is unrepentant and unchanged by the fact that he must now face his death, his moment of judgment. He has no regard for his soul when he cries out for Jesus to save him. He is only looking for an escape, a way out of this helpless situation. He is not asking for a new life or a second chance to make good. He is not even afraid to die. He is just angry that he's being punished.

"Are you not the Christ?" (Luke 23:39) he says, railing at Jesus. Behind his words, there is more doubt than belief. His words are loaded with all the wrong expectations of what the Savior should be and do. Although it may well have been within His abilities, Jesus would not call upon the angels of God to rescue him. His purpose is not to wield power in some self-serving way. Rather, just as He has shown the world how to live through the example of His life, He is showing the world how to die by sacrificing Himself.

"Save yourself and us" (Luke 23:29b). The criminal echoes the scoffing of the pharisees when they said, "He saved others; let Him save Himself, if He is the Christ of God, His chosen one" (Luke 23:35). His words echo the mocking of the soldiers who say the same: "If you are the king of the Jews, save yourself" (v. 37). The prisoner was just joining the crowd, adding insult to injury. But the meaning of salvation is so much more than their vision of a physical rescue. It's a spiritual life that reveals a kingdom that knows only love and goodness, only peace and compassion, only service and joy, and only truth and faith. By saving Himself from His own death, He could save no one from his or her sins, for it is by His death that we are forgiven. By saving Himself through some kind of outward show of infinite power, no one would ever *need* to have faith. But it is by faith that we are saved. It is through trust that we are able to pass from death to life in Christ. And it is by believing that we are made new. Our God is not a God who evokes goodness or obedience because we witness some spectacular use of power. Our God is not separate from us, casting out orders from on high. Our God loves us and touches us and fills us with His Spirit so we may witness His kingdom even now. *Today*, you will be with me in paradise (Luke 23:43).

But not unless you give up the bitterness and anger and false images of power, wanting to control your fate by insisting that the power of God should come to serve you at your call. One of the men beside Jesus was made bitter by the pain of life. But the other man's eyes were opened by it. Perhaps all of his pain was summed up in one moment for this man, and rather than anger, he felt remorse; rather than denial, he accepted his guilt and he was sorry. Perhaps he was afraid of the eternal consequences facing him in this his moment of judgement. "Do you not fear God?" (v. 40). Is he speaking only to the other criminal who has just railed at Christ out of desperation and defiance, or do you hear him speaking to his crucifiers and the scoffers too? "Do you not fear God, since you are under the same condemnation?" Do you hear him speaking to you?

Admitting his guilt, he says, "We indeed are being condemned justly" (Luke 23:40). Where are you on that spectrum of guilt and innocence? Are you closer to condemnation for your deeds, or have you done nothing wrong? I tend to believe that those who think they have done nothing wrong have probably actually done nothing at all.

But here, this man is bearing witness to the truth in a way that not even Jesus's closest disciples had the courage to proclaim: that of the innocence of Christ! It seems as if he knew Him somehow. Had he seen Him teach? Had he been close by when He went through the questioning of Pilate? Did he see the falseness of the plot against Him? Had he heard Pilate say that he had found no guilt in Him? Somehow, this criminal even knew His name: "Jesus, remember me when you come into your kingdom" (v. 42).

Remember me. Jesus once told a parable (Matthew 20:1–16) about how the kingdom of heaven is like a householder who hired laborers to work in his vineyard. Some, he hired at the beginning of the day, some, halfway through the morning, some at noon, some a little later, and some near the very end of the day. But he paid them all the same. He remembered the workers he had hired and the amount he had promised to give each one. But some, who had been working in the vineyard all day, resented that those who had worked for such a short time got paid the same. Jesus ends the story by telling his hearers that the householder says, "Do you begrudge my generosity?" And then Jesus says, "so the last shall be first, and the first last" (vv. 15b–16).

Remember me. This criminal was the last person Jesus saved in His earthly manifestation. He was the last laborer in the vineyard, but the first to be paid. Why? Because everyone who is faithful is remembered equally well by God. "Remember me when you come into your kingdom" (v. 42). His is an appeal for mercy that proclaims not only the kingdom of Christ, but that Christ is the king. It is a statement of the very belief that is being denied by his crucifiers, the very belief for which Jesus has been condemned, that he is a king. The kingdom of Christ. The last man to be saved by the living Jesus was the first to be paid because his humility was the greatest: he was dying on a cross. He was least of the laborers but also many times as desperate, and the most undeserving receive the most mercy in the kingdom of Christ. To those furthest from grace, God is most gracious in the kingdom of Christ.

The penitent man on the cross beside Christ is restored in that instant; he is redeemed immediately by the faith of his plea. He is pardoned for his crimes and forgiven of his sins. Perhaps he had heard Jesus's words as he prayed for his executioners, saying, "Father, forgive them" (v. 34). There, he saw the mercy of God and he knew his shame in comparison. He knew his utter desolation without Christ. He knew how lost he really was, and he knew his need. He simply asked to be remembered, to be thought of from the point of view of the kingdom of God.

And just as in prayer, we might ask God to remember the poor, we would not just ask for them merely to be thoughts in the divine mind, but to be considered in their needs and that their needs might be met. So, likewise, the man on the cross makes a request for his need. He is asking, out of consideration for his desperate need, to be remembered with mercy.

And his humble request is met far beyond his expectations. Jesus doesn't condemn the man. He doesn't offer just an inkling of hope, and He doesn't just forgive him! He gives him the promise of eternity. He treats him not only as a sinner for whom He would give His life, but as a companion of His kingdom. A companion He would choose.

"Truly, I say to you, today, you will be with me in paradise" (v. 43). Today, Jesus does not suggest that it will happen at some future day at the end of time. It will happen today! All too often, we get caught up in the belief that everyone who dies has to go to some kind of holding place before his or her moment of judgment. But the moment of judgment for this man, whose name is never revealed, is even before his death, because he is dying with his judge. He is dying with his king. The presence of the kingdom has been revealed ever since the coming of Christ. We are not to believe that eternity begins at some particular point in time. That would make it less than eternity, which exists beyond time. But the moment of death is the moment of judgment. And the moment of judgment is when we face the eternal God and find the beginning of either eternal life or eternal death.

But the beginning of paradise, of heaven, of eternal life is not yet for this man on the cross beside Jesus because he speaks in the future tense: "You *will be* with me" (v. 43). It is a promise. Salvation is now—today. It is a feeling of belonging. "You will be with me!" And it is the promise of paradise.

Eternal life begins now, my friends. It begins when we turn to Christ in penitential shame and appeal to Him to remember us, to consider our needs. And though we know we are unworthy of His consideration, for we are far from Him in our sinfulness, we trust His graciousness. And He Is telling us that *today*, we can be with Him in paradise. It's so easy. It's so simple. It is so free because He's so accepting, so merciful, and so kind that He would die to save our souls!

A Prayer

Almighty God, today is the day. Help us seize the day with the same trust as the penitential thief on the cross beside Jesus. Help us acknowledge that You have a glorious kingdom and that you would welcome us into it. As we ask for You to remember us, help us to remember you before others who may need to be reminded that the first step toward You is the beginning of our entrance into Your Kingdom. This we pray in Jesus' anime. Amen.

Why Have You Forsaken Me?

From noon on, darkness came over the whole land
until three in the afternoon.
And about three o'clock, Jesus cried with a loud voice,
"Eli, Eli, lema sabachthani?"
That is, "My God, my God, why have you forsaken me?"
(Matthew 27:45–46)

The darkness is never deepest until it is entered into from the brilliance of a light so divine as to set fire to the hearts of men and women whenever it is revealed. As Jesus Christ, the light of the world, is crucified and dying, they were plunged into the deepest hour of darkness the world would ever know. "From the sixth hour there was darkness over all the earth until the ninth hour. And about the ninth hour Jesus cried, 'My God, my God, Why have you forsaken me?'" (Matthew 27:45–46).

Why? This is the eternal question. Why did God give up His only Son? Why did Jesus have to die? Why did the messiah have to suffer so? Why? Because God loves the world. Why did Jesus have to die? Because God wanted to forgive the world. Why did the messiah have to suffer as He did? To help us to believe. You see, it's not just Jesus on the cross; it's God. Jesus Christ is God incarnate, the Word made flesh. How far are you willing to go to convince someone of the truth?

Why have *you* forsaken me? Did God forsake Himself? Did God turn away or hide from His own flesh? Is God masked from His purpose in Christ at His own moment of judgment? Is *this* a moment of judgment? Yes and no. Yes, God relinquished His power, forsaking Himself out of love for you and me. But no, God also reserved His power to manifest it more purely in the Resurrection. Yes, God did turn away and hide from His own flesh to manifest, in His own self-sacrifice, in His own death, the faith that is love, the dedication that is trust, and the sacrifice that is loyalty. He died to save us because He loved us. But then, no, God did not hide Himself from His own flesh; He revealed Himself. In one and the same moment, God is masked and made visible; Jesus is forsaken and refortified, for as much as this moment is His moment of judgment, His ultimate trial, so is it the moment of judgment for the whole world. "And this is the judgment, that the light has come into the world, and men loved darkness rather than light, because their deeds were evil" (John 3:19).

Is Jesus forsaken by God? Or is it that Christ feels the very human feeling of aloneness? He was deserted and denied by His disciples, convicted as a criminal, sentenced as a sinner, mocked by the very people who need Him most but who deny Him so absolutely. Betrayed, beaten, and broken, Jesus was forsaken by His own fellow human. What other human experience could make us feel anything other than forsaken by God? Even with the promise before us that there is nothing that shall ever separate us from His love—not tribulation or distress or persecution or famine or nakedness or peril or sword; neither death, nor life, nor angels, nor principalities, nor things present, nor things to come, nor powers, nor height, nor depth, nor anything else in all creation will be able to separate us from the love of God (Romans 8:35, 38–39). Even with this promise etched upon our hearts, the feeling is real. And Jesus feels forsaken.

Why have you forsaken *me*? (Matthew 27:46). Me, the Son God loves! "As the Father has loved me, so have I loved you" (John 15:9). This is the one God sent to reveal His very love of the world. This is God's chosen and precious, the very stone that the builders rejected that was to become the chief of the corner (Mark 12:10). This, God has forsaken!

As much as Christ has taught that, where your treasure is, there will your heart be also, (Matthew 6:21), so is Jesus the treasure, the very heart of God. God is giving His heart for the sake of the world. For what would you give your heart? What is the risk you would take out of love? What fearful deed, what depth of sorrow would you be willing to go through to convince the world of your love?

"Why hast thou forsaken me?" (Matthew 27:46), Christ cries. Is it out of self-pity? Is it in sorrow? Is it in fear? Or is it surrender? Jesus, the man, is dying without the use of power that Jesus, the Son of God, possesses. Suffering alone, in an ultimate way. Lost, forlorn. Wounded. Forsaken. Defenseless. Surrendered.

"Why hast thou *forsaken* me?" (Matthew 27:46). Alone. Lonely. Forgotten. Left behind. Abandoned. The world had given up on Jesus, hardened its heart, and cursed the only one that could save them. Not God too!

How have *you* forgotten Jesus Christ? How have you left Him behind? How have you abandoned your Savior? How have you forgotten to worship? How have you left your faith behind? How have you abandoned the church?

The church is the body of Christ! Its purpose is to continue what Jesus began. Its purpose is to be in the world but not of the world. It is not a retirement home for people who have been good. It's more of a hospital for sinners, broken and in need of healing. Just like Jesus, who ate and drank with sinners, it is here, not to be served, but to serve (Matthew 20:28). And if it is thought of primarily as a "sacred" place, then, what am *I* doing here? I am in search of the sacred. I am in need of the sacred. I am desperate for the sacred, but the church is not opened to keep people out. It is not in the world for people to escape. It is here to save the world! God loves the world and would serve the world by whatever means of grace might be needed, but the people in the church all too often limit the ministry of grace. Perhaps their expectations of the church are different from mine or of church officials or of Christ. After all, the church *is* His body (1 Corinthians 12:27).

Why is the church abandoned? Because Jesus Christ is abandoned. Why is the church left behind? Because Jesus Christ is left behind. Because Jesus Christ is forgotten. Jesus is abandoned whenever anyone else is abandoned. How have you been abandoned? How have you been left behind? How have you been forgotten? How is the church forgotten?

The feeling is very real. And we can all begin to wonder with Christ if even God has abandoned us. But the promise that calls us is the promise proclaimed by Paul—that nothing shall separate us from the love of God.

To feel forsaken, sometimes, is to feel like nothing. But nothing shall separate us from the love of God. And because I'm not nothing, but something, and because you're not nothing, but something, our purpose, the purpose of God in Christ, in our hearts, is to reverse the separation process. To bring people together, to bring the love of God (Matthew 27:46).

A Prayer

Almighty God, sometimes we can feel forgotten, forsaken. We can feel like nobody cares. But You care. We are *not* forsaken. There is always a thread of purpose tying us to Your will, to Your life. Please, live in us, in our hearts and minds, in our hope. Give us such a sense of Your everlasting love that we are renewed by the thought of You. And help us always remember You to others that they may have the confidence that is faith and the determination that is Your way. This we pray in Jesus' name. Amen.

I Thirst

After this, when Jesus knew that all was now finished,
he said (in order to fulfill the scriptures),
"I am thirsty."
(John 19:28)

There is a longing of the heart, an aching desire, the depth of which reveals an intensity that can only be described as a truly great thirst. And yet many people languish. They may not even know it, but they are spiritually dry. What is it that can refresh them? How can they be brought to a longing for faith that is as strong as a thirsty person's longing for water?

Each one of us suffers some kind of emotional or spiritual thirst. We are made that way. Should we cease to long for something more or something greater, some depth yet unknown, our lives would simply seem to be over. But it's not over until it's over. The moment we have accomplished one goal, another goal looms up before us because time keeps coming and something new keeps happening. Sometimes that goal might even be to live one more day, to breathe one more hour, to taste life one more time. We are never complete until God is finished with us. To be human, to be alive, is to want, to need, to desire.

Here is a very human Jesus, dying of thirst, suffering the agony of crucifixion, not just beginning to see the coming of the shadow of death, but deep in its valley. This is the Good Shepherd. To follow Him is to know no want; to know Him is to find a peace as calm as if led beside still waters; to serve Him is to know the blessing of a cup running over (Psalm 23). This, the Good Shepherd, is dry, empty, dying, thirsting, and wanting. Here is the thirsty messiah, who would have offered living water to any who ask: "Whoever drinks of the water that I shall give will never thirst; the water that I shall give will become a spring within welling up to eternal life" (John 4:14).

Thirst is a great threat to life. So, likewise, the spiritually dry are perishing eternally. We thirst for and desire all the wrong things, and still, we are empty. Still, something is missing, and the desire created by that lack, that thirst, leaves us weak. Paul has said, "My strength is made perfect in weakness" (2 Corinthians 12:9). What thirst leaves you weak? What is your heart's desire? What is your most-intense ambition? Is it to be happy? To be blessed? "Blessed are those who hunger and thirst for righteousness, for they shall be satisfied" (Matthew 5:6).

In that one beatitude, Jesus proclaims the only drink that truly quenches our deepest thirst. Jesus promises fullness for those who are spiritually dry, if only they know their true thirst, the right desire. The blessing comes because of the desire, not the attainment of what is desired; because if you desire something enough, you will work hard to get it. And then you will work hard to keep it. You will sacrifice everything to get it, to keep it, to quench your thirst.

Jesus says, "I am thirsty" (John 19:28). He's suffering. Suffering for my sins. Suffering in my place. His body is poured out like water (Psalm 22:14) for us. He wants. He needs. In his need is a desire, and His desire is to be relieved. But He knows that He must drink the cup that the Father has given Him (John 18:11). He knows that His only relief will come when it is over—when it is finished. His thirst is not for water only, but for God. For what do you thirst?

We're all thirsty. Before us lies an ocean full of the wrong kind of water. But we soon learn that if we drink its salt water, the thirst remains and grows. We need to move inland, inward, searching for the spring of pure water that truly quenches. There's a well; there's a fountain of life that's been uncovered. It's just waiting to be tapped, and it's here in our midst. It's here in our hearts. It's flowing among us. It is love. It's a love so sweet and so simple that Jesus would say that "whoever gives you a cup of cold water to drink because you bear the name of Christ, will by no means lose the reward" (Mark 9:41). Who is the unnamed person who saw the bowl of vinegar nearby and took a sponge saturated with the drink on the end of a stalk of hyssop to hold it to His mouth for Jesus to drink? Who is it? Is it you? "I was thirsty, and you gave me drink" (Matthew 25:35b), He said. "As you did it to one of the least of these, my brethren, you did it unto me. (Matthew 25:40). Are you thirsty like Christ? Come. Take. Eat. Drink. He is with you.

A Prayer

Almighty God, Your power is made perfect in weakness. At your most vulnerable moment as Jesus, You suffered. I feel Your pain. I understand Your thirst. And You understand my thirst, my suffering. All I ask is for comfort. All I really need is for my vulnerability to be brought before Your mercy. Please, hear my prayer. Amen.

It Is Finished

When Jesus had received the wine, He said,
"It is finished."
Then He bowed His head and gave up His spirit.
(John 19:30)

In the story "The Quest" by Ray Bradbury, a child is born to a tribe of people who live in a dark sort of inner underworld where their full life span lasts only eight days. They grow from infancy to old age in that briefness of time because, since they are in the darkness, their hearts are racing. The child is immediately taken from its parents, and his training begins. By the third day, he has been trained and is now ready for his quest. At the end of his difficult journey toward a slim source of light, there lies a great, massive gate that his people believe he can open. If he can, the light will come into their darkness, and their lives will change.

As his quest unfolds, the boy encounters various obstacles that his training helps him to overcome. But all too soon, he discovers that he is growing old. He must continue on. He must finish his quest. He must struggle to reach the gate. And when he finally does, old and tired, and it opens for him, the light enters into the world of his people, and immediately, every heartbeat softens its pace. Life now will seem so much fuller, less hurried, more complete. It becomes a whole new world for them. They will never be the same.

It is finished. His quest was finished when the gate was opened and the light entered into that dark world of hopeless existence. His quest was finished, but its end was just the beginning.

The last words of Jesus Christ before His Resurrection in the gospel of John are, "It is finished!" Jesus had likewise opened a great door. But this door is the door of forgiveness, of salvation, of eternal life. We can never be the same unless we refuse to see the light.

Imagine completing a course. The class is finished, but God isn't finished with any of us yet. Jesus could say, "It is finished," only because the redeeming work of salvation was complete in His suffering and death on the cross. But that's not the end of the story!

After the gate had been opened in the Ray Bradbury story, the people now had to begin a whole new outlook on life. The boy who opened the gate stepped through it into a whole new world, where life was more abundant, and the darkness was defeated. Here we are, born into a world where the light is already shining. The quest has already been completed. The gate has long since been opened. What must we do now? What is our quest?

A similar question was once asked of Jesus: "What shall I do to inherit eternal life?" (Luke 10:25). It's like saying, "What do I need to be complete?" Or "What do I need to be able to say, 'It is finished'?" The answer has to do with love. "Love the Lord your God with all your heart, and with all your soul, and with all your strength, and with all your mind, and love your neighbor as yourself" (Luke 10:27).

If the question becomes about how, the answer can be seen all across the holy scriptures. But first of all, the concluding verses of the parable of the Good Samaritan give some clues: Which of these three, do you think, proved to be a neighbor to the man who fell among robbers? The one who showed mercy on him. Jesus said, go and do likewise.

"Loving your neighbor" does not ask who, but rather how. Anyone who needs you is your neighbor. You must be the one who responds. But still, "How?" remains and Jesus gives an answer in the parable of the Great Judgment in Matthew 25. This also gives some clues as to how to love God: "I was hungry, and you gave me food; I was thirsty, and you gave me drink; I was a stranger and you welcomed me; I was naked, and you clothed me; I was sick and you visited me; I was in prison and you came to me" (vv. 35–36). The question becomes,

"When was it you, Lord?" (vv. 37–39). The answer is, "as you did it to one of the least of these my brethren, you did it unto me" (v. 40).

Nothing is finished until it is perfect. Nothing is complete until it is perfect. Love is not complete until it serves neighbors, until it serves the least of the brothers and sisters of Christ. Love is patient and kind, not jealous or boastful, or arrogant or rude. Love does not insist on its own way. Love does not rejoice in the wrong, but rejoices in the right. Love becomes complete when it can bear all things, believe all things, hope all things, and endure all things. And when love becomes perfect, it never ends (1 Corinthians 13:4–8a). We may think we have all the faith we need, but, without the love that serves even the least of people, we are nothing (1 Corinthians 13:2). Without love, we are unfinished. Without love, we cannot be perfect.

And there's our ongoing quest: when the perfect comes, the imperfect will pass (1 Corinthians 13:10). Our task is to finish our faith, to complete it, to perfect it. To work out our own salvation in fear and trembling (Philippians 2:12). In 1 John 2:5, we are told of Christ that whoever keeps His word, in Him truly love for God is perfected. Inasmuch as you did it to one of the least of these … (Matthew 25:40). And the writer of Hebrews tells us to, "Lay aside every weight, and sin which clings so closely, and let us run with perseverance the race that is set before us, looking to Jesus, the pioneer and perfecter of our faith, who for the joy that was set before him endured the cross …" (Hebrews 12:1–2). "Although he was a son, he learned obedience through his suffering; and being made perfect, he became the source of eternal salvation to all who obey him" (Hebrews 5:9). "By this we know love, that he laid down his life for us; and we ought to lay down our lives for the brethren" (1 John 3:16). "If we love one another, God abides in us, and His love is perfected in us" (1 John 4:12). "In this is love perfected with us, that we may have confidence for the day of judgment, because as he is, so are we in this world. We must not be afraid to be like Jesus, to sacrifice a little for the sake of others. "There is no fear in love, but perfect love casts out fear" (1 John 4:17–18).

And Jesus said, "It is finished" (John 19:30). He opened the gate, but we must walk through. He revealed the light, but we must see it with our hearts. He taught the truth, but we must believe it. He showed the way, but we must follow. And He set the example by His life, but we must live as He lived and do as He did. He has given us the tools, and we must finish the work.

One of Christ's greatest disciples was a man who hated Him at first. Paul changed, though. We can all change. Jesus Christ changes us. Faith finishes us. Paul discovered a new treasure, and his heart was reborn. Paul discovered that where his treasure is, there could his heart be also (Matthew 6:19). In a way he discovered his heart by discovering the true treasure. And at the end of his journey, in his second letter to Timothy (4:6–7), he sort of echoed the words of Christ on the cross: "I am already at the point of being sacrificed; the time of my departure has come. I have fought the good fight, I have finished the race, I have kept the faith."

Jesus came to perfect us in love. And until we can truly love, we are not finished. The work of Christ has not ended either, though it is complete, perfect, finished. It has not ended because He is still working in us, through us, and among us by His Spirit, revealing again and again what it is to love. And it is His own words that we must hear (John 15:12–14): "This is my commandment, that you love one another as I have loved you. Greater love has no man than this, that a man lay down his life for his friends. You are my friends if you do what I command you …"

It is finished. And we have just begun!

A Prayer

Almighty God, You are not finished with any of us yet. You didn't bring us this far just to bring us this far. Be with us to help us finish the race, to reach the goal, to discover the prize till we are truly perfected in love. This we pray in Jesus' name. Amen,

Into Your Hands

It was now about noon,
and darkness came over the whole land until three in the afternoon,
while the sun's light failed;
and the curtain of the temple was torn in two.
Then Jesus, crying with a loud voice, said,
"Father, into your hands I commend my spirit."
Having said this, he breathed his last.
(Luke 23:44–46)

In the gospel of Luke, in the final dying words of Christ, are you able to see the confidence? Do you see the trust of a son? Do you see the assurance of that closest of relationships? Do you see the strength of conviction that knows no room for doubt? Do you see the dedication, the act of utter dependence, the certainty, the reliance upon God? Do you see the faith? Right here, in these seven final words, Jesus Christ, who revealed by His example the life of faith, is now revealing the *death* of faith. Jesus Christ has not only shown us how to live; He has shown us how to die.

Father, into your hands I commend my spirit (Luke 23:46). To whom does our spirit belong in the first place? From where has our life come? Whose are we that we could do no less? Whose are we that we should ever think we were our own? All too often, we live as though there was no one to account to. As if there was no real power over us and we ourselves were in control. These words of Christ remind us that it is always God who rules. Though God has no hands, the power is His, as if it was in His hands. Christ's words

237

remind us that we belong to God. Not as pets, not as toys, but as children in His family, as subjects in His kingdom, as servants of His will. And every time we neglect these facts, this relationship, we cease to do God's will and begin to lose our way.

But Jesus Christ never did less than entrust His life to the Father. He relied constantly and completely upon God for His life's purpose. "I have come down from heaven, not to do my own will, but the will of him who sent me" (John 6:38). God's will was always what Jesus willed. And in Jesus Christ, God's image and likeness, the fullness of God was pleased to dwell (Colossians 1:19. ESV), not as an effect of Christ's reliance on His Father, but as a result of God's love. And for us, it is when we commit our lives to God that we begin to change into His image. His love begins to work in us, through us, and among us because this sort of commitment is an act of love, of trust, of devotion.

How many of us claim that love, profess that trust, and declare that devotion, but forgo any outward signs of commitment? How then, will we die? How, then, will we experience heaven? I would suggest that, should we live with the intention of being truly faithful, in the final analysis, we will experience God's intention for us and only His intention. There is a difference between entering into heaven's glory, and knowing that God had intended glory for us. Just as there is a difference between intending to go to church and actually going to church, commitment, real commitment, walks through the door!

Into your hands I commend my spirit (Luke 23:46). Such commitment is to God's kingdom. It is when we give ourselves to Christ that we become heaven's citizens, and it is when we are no longer our own in any way that we discover its eternal nature in our lives. It is when we have truly taken the leap of faith, trusting sincerely that God's hands are waiting, that we find God's hands were always there.

There is a commitment that is devotion, that is service, that is active in its expression. But there is also a commitment that is surrender. But it does not mean giving up. It is more of a submission, a relinquishment, a renunciation, a yielding. It is Thomas saying,

"Let us also go, that we may die with him" (John 11:16). It is Peter saying, "Lord, I will lay down my life for you" (John 14:37). It is Jesus saying, "No one takes (my life) from me, but I have power to lay it down" (John 10:18). And it is Jesus saying, "Not my will, but thine be done" (Luke 22:42). This is the commitment that is surrender. It is a commitment that is sacrifice.

There is a virtue in such selflessness, but it comes by a sense of commitment that goes all the way and does not give up. There was Jesus Christ, suffering, dying, depending on God to carry Him in His death as He carried Him in His life, relying on God not to let go when He entered the darkness of the tomb. Committing Himself to the divine will a final time, believing, trusting that God would raise Him up and give Him a new, unending life, a life empowered by the pureness of God's love.

And it's a life that somehow we are invited to be a part of. By committing our lives to the life of Christ, by giving our lives, by entrusting our spirits to Him, by living with Jesus Christ, we will rise with Jesus Christ. By entering into God's heavenly kingdom now, through commitment, we will find a place prepared for us, an everlasting home. Jesus said in John 11:25, "I am the Resurrection and the life; they who believe in me, though they die, yet shall they live; and whosoever lives and believes in me shall never die."

It is well that this book ends with the words of Christ commending His Spirit into the hands of God. We must do so as well.

It is enough!

Printed in the United States
by Baker & Taylor Publisher Services